T0208339

FROM GLORY TO GLORY

MELODIE ROMEO

BALBOA.
PRESS
A DIVISION OF HAY HOUSE

Balboa Press books may be ordered through booksellers or by contacting:

Balboa Press
A Division of Hay House
1663 Liberty Drive
Bloomington, IN 47403
www.balboapress.com
1 (877) 407-4847

Print information available on the last page.

ISBN: 978-1-9822-3146-0 (sc)
ISBN: 978-1-9822-3149-1 (e)

Balboa Press rev. date: 07/19/2019

CONTENTS

INTRODUCTION

After years of being a musician, teacher, writer, farmer, and every avocation imaginable, life pushed me into a career choice where I could actually make money. So for the past four and a half years I have been traversing America as an over-the-road truck driver. I am pleased to be paying off bills and preparing for retirement, but it is an extremely boring job. At first I joked about getting paid to listen to the radio, but fourteen-hour days, seven days a week only getting home once every four to six weeks can be grueling; it also affords an abundance of time to listen to audio books, think, meditate, and pray. I began to sing in earnest the worship songs on my CDs: "Open the eyes of my heart, Lord, I want to see you;" (Michael W. Smith) "More love, more power, more of You in my life. And I will worship You, with all of my heart; I will worship You, with all of my mind, I will worship You with all of my strength, For You are my Lord;" (Michael W. Smith) "In the secret, in the quiet place, In the stillness you are there; In the secret, in the quiet hour I wait only for you, Cause I want to know you more. I want to know you, I want to hear your voice, I want to know you more. I want to touch you, I want to see your face, I want to know you more." (Darlene Zschech, Hillsong) I believe the Lord heard the calling of my heart and answered.

Have you ever had a "glory" experience, one where a light bulb came on? Maybe it was an encounter with God or a sudden realization of some great truth. There are many more such "glory" experiences just waiting for you! Along the road God has opened my heart and mind to deep spiritual truths that I had never been taught but once seen make perfect sense.

I've spent about a year just getting comfortable with them and trying to organize the onslaught of new and powerful ideas. Throughout history new revelations have been added to the old as we strive to obtain a fuller understanding of God and spirituality. As stated in 2 Corinthians 3:18, *And we all, who with unveiled faces contemplate the Lord's glory, are being transformed into His image with ever increasing glory, which comes from the Lord, who is the Spirit.* (NIV) The King James Version uses the phrase "being transformed from glory to glory". I fully understand this passage. God rewards those who diligently seek Him (Hebrews 11:6) regardless of their religious affiliation or lack thereof, and He is continuing to show us new truths as we are open to receive them. As my spirit and mind have been quickened with fresh comprehension, I have truly been lifted from glory to glory and feel the urgent need to share, as best I can, what I have experienced and incorporated into my understanding of the universe.

From the beginning I wish to make clear that I have not cornered the market on all knowledge. I do not claim to have the answer to every question nor the sole source of all truth. Anyone who thinks he/she knows it all, is either a liar or a fool. And for one known as a wordsmith, I am experiencing unprecedented difficulties expressing the insights that have manifested themselves to me. Some of the conclusions I have reached may seem a bridge too far for many. But perhaps at least one concept in this volume will speak to you, and if I can bless one person in any way through this effort, it is not in vain.

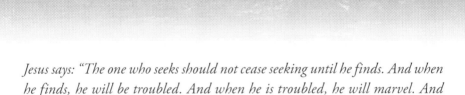

WHO IS GOD?

Jesus says: "The one who seeks should not cease seeking until he finds. And when he finds, he will be troubled. And when he is troubled, he will marvel. And he will reign over all." The Gospel of Thomas, 2:1-4[1]

I remember the moment, what was said and how I felt as if it just happened, although I'm a bit fuzzy on many of the details such as the date or year. As I recall, I was in Grade 8 or 9 walking through the fellowship hall of First Baptist Church with a group of my friends going from one youth activity to another. I was - and still am - a nerd who always tried to surround myself with the smartest people I could find. Therefore, it was completely natural that in the course of our conversation a scientific discovery would come up. One of my friends said, "Hey, did you hear

---

[1] The Gospel of Thomas is a collection of sayings of Jesus in the tradition of the Jewish teachers of wisdom. When the Council of Nicaea met in 325 under the direction of Constantine I to codify a more concise collection of texts into what we call the Bible, they omitted 45 letters, gospels, and supporting documents that were widely circulated among early church congregations, such as the Gospel of Thomas. The manuscript resurfaced in Nag Hammadi Egypt in 1945 when thirteen codices were discovered buried in clay jars where the sacred texts had been hidden in the mid-forth century for safe keeping. Many scholars consider them to be as legitimate as any books that were chosen for inclusion in the Bible by the Council of Nicaea.

about this quantum energy field? They aren't sure if it is made up of waves or particles, but they say it's everywhere connecting everything, and that it is what holds the atoms together. Scientists don't know what it is and can't even agree on what to call it, but isn't that far out?"

Casually, without missing a beat, I shrugged. "I know what that is." This caused the group to stop in their tracks and stare at me. It was truly not my intention to be an insufferable know-it-all, although I can see how that may have appeared to be the case. I just knew, as if I had somehow always known without anyone telling me, and it seemed as obvious as a flashing neon sign. "It's God. Scientists have just discovered God."

It was a metamorphic revelation, tremendous beyond comparison, and yet it felt like someone proclaiming that the sky was blue. Being a young teen with so many other things to do and think about, I tucked that truly astounding revelation away and didn't give it a second thought–for over forty years. Then I came across scientist turned author and lecturer Gregg Braden and his book "The Divine Matrix," and suddenly it all clicked.

There is only one God, but that Power is called by many names. When Moses asked the entity in the burning bush who spoke, the reply came, "I am that I am." Every religion and tradition on earth has given a name to the Divine Creator: Yahweh, Jehovah, El Shaddai, Elohim, Elyon, Allah, Khuda, All Mighty, All Glorious, Baha, Great Spirit, Supreme Being, Parambrahma, and hundreds of others. The key thing to understand is that the major faiths of the world all acknowledge the *same* God; they just use different names. Even Hinduism, which may appear to be polytheistic, recognizes one supreme deity. Likewise, many Native American and indigenous traditions which include forms of animism still call upon a Creator or Great Spirit.

"Oh," you think; "You're one of those Universalists." No, not as such. What I am telling you is there is One God, the Creator of Heaven and earth, the Lord over all the universe, but He did not create a religion. Humans produced the concept of religion, possibly as a way to organize ideas and possibly as a way to control their populations. The majority of world belief systems are simply formed around different ways to acknowledge and/or worship the same One God, and while we may disagree on how that is done, it does not make one way *right* and another way *wrong*.

I want you to pause a moment and think about this fact: God created the

Heavens and the earth, but God did not create or establish an institution of religion. He did make a covenant with Abraham, but that was a relationship, not a religion. God did give Moses the Ten Commandments, but that was a guideline, not a religion. The religion of Judaism was built around these two as were its offshoots of Christianity and Islam. So, what *does* God say about religion? The Bible rarely uses that term, but two New Testament passages make clear what God says religion should be. *But if a widow has children or grandchildren, these should learn first of all to put their religion into practice by caring for their own family and so repaying their parents and grandparents, for this is pleasing to God.* (1 Timothy 5:4, NIV) *Those who consider themselves religious and yet do not keep a tight rein on their tongues deceive themselves, and their religion is worthless. Religion that God our Father accepts as pure and faultless is this: to look after orphans and widows in their distress and to keep oneself from being polluted by the world.* (James 1:26, 27, NIV)

While man's construct of religion is based on belief systems, practices, rituals, attending certain gatherings, and obeying certain rules, the actual words of the scriptures make it clear that God's definition of religion is based on how we treat other people, particularly children, the elderly, and those less fortunate than ourselves. Many Christian denominations talk about their faith as being a relationship rather than a religion, but then fall back into the same religious trappings as those who do not give voice to that distinction. We must unlearn what we have learned and free ourselves from restrictive thought and divisive postures.

Does this mean we should forsake our beliefs and stop attending our churches, temples, synagogues, mosques, and meeting houses? Certainly not. As a group, congregations of faith can engage in greater service ministries than one person alone and they provide a necessary social support group. If done properly, they offer an atmosphere of worship and place to expand our knowledge. But if done poorly they inhibit, limit, and stifle growth, even leading people away from God rather than toward Him. Jesus warned us not to be deceived by false prophets and the people He chastised the most were the religious leaders of His day because they were not teaching truth nor acting in love. God is not concerned with what label you hang over your door; He is concerned with how you treat people of the earth, His very own beloved children.

God is Spirit; but what is spirit? The dictionary provides several definitions including: *the principle of conscious life; the incorporeal part of humans; the vital principle in humans, animating the body or mediating between body and soul; conscious, incorporeal being; a supernatural, incorporeal being; a divine, inspiring, or animating being or influence.* More simply put, a spirit is a living, conscious entity that we can't see with our eyes or touch with our hands but is nevertheless present.

Because of our limited ability to comprehend, we usually think of God in human terms, most notably applying the masculine pronoun "he". While I will use that pronoun in this treatise because "it" seems disrespectful, I would be just as correct to say "she." The Holy Book of the Great Invisible Spirit 41:6-6 (also part of the Nag Hammadi library) states, *Three powers came forth from the Great Invisible Spirit: the Father, the Mother, and the Child.* And Genesis 1:27 (NIV) declares, *So God created mankind in his own image, in the image of God he created them; male and female he created them.* God is not male or female, but both - a complete being displaying aspects of both genders. We see God as life-giver, a female role, and protector, a masculine one; nurturer and judge, beautiful and strong. God is a spirit, not to be confused with a mortal, and is just as much female as male. I will also use the common name "God" throughout this writing, although Allah, Yahweh, or Parambrahma are just as legitimate.

You are in the sunshine,
You are in the rain;
You are in the snow that falls
On mountaintops and plains.

I hear You in the thunder
And the whisper on the wind;
You are my Creator,
And You are my friend.

I find You in the congregation
Or in silent solitude;
I see You in a mother hen,
Wings spread o'er her brood.

You reside on distant stars
And the deepest ocean blue;
You live in all creation,
And all creation lives in you.
A poem by Melodie Romeo

Some people have this image of God as an old man with a white beard sitting upon a cloud with a stick in one hand and a carrot in the other–nothing could be farther from the truth! No matter what your image of God, I am writing this to tell you He is SO much bigger, SO much more powerful, SO much more awesome than the wildest imaginings of the mortal mind. We have been taught that God is omnipresent (everywhere at the same time) and omnipotent (all powerful) without truly appreciating what that means. I will attempt to explain in a way the reader can understand.

Max Planck, Nobel Prize winning quantum physicist, was a contemporary of Albert Einstein and made unprecedented discoveries. In a speech he gave in Florence, Italy in 1944 he revealed his most remarkable conclusion, that as a man devoted to science and the study of physics, he at last had determined that matter and the atom do not exist as we think they do, but though a force that brings atomic particles together and holds them in place. He determined this could only be achieved by a conscious intelligence that makes up the matrix of all things.

Remember when we were all in school and learned about atoms? Our textbooks said the atom was the smallest particle of matter, except for the tiny elements that made up the atom–protons, neutrons, and electrons. Using high powered electron microscopes and particle excellerators physicists have now discovered that not only do atoms not actually look like we were taught, but there is a smaller particle that forms the electrons, neutrons, and protons. This now tiniest known particle is called a photon, and a photon is a minute particle of light, thereby proving one of Einstein's theories from 1905. So let's think about this for just a moment. In Genesis 1:3 *God said, "Let there be light," and there was light.* Now we discover that all things in our universe are made up of photons which are tiny particles of light!

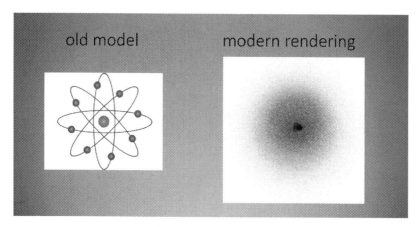

Two images of Atoms

Pythagoras, Aristotle, and other ancient Greek scientists and philosophers taught a fifth element besides fire, water, air, and earth—ether (or aether). This ether was the substance that filled the entire universe, so in their understanding there was no empty space. Western scientists widely held this belief until the apparent failure of the famous Michelson–Morley experiment of 1887. The experiment tried to prove the existence of the ether field by measuring the effects it might have on light. Using the tools available to them at the time the two scientists were disappointed to not see the results they expected. At that point the scientific community dismissed the idea of the field and declared space to be void and nothing to be connected to anything else. But in 1986 a physicist named E. W. Silvertooth repeated the Michelson–Morley experiment with modern equipment which was far more sophisticated and this time the results supported the existence of this ether wind or stream providing a different explanation of how light moves through space than the one proposed by Einstein.

While not all physicists agree, what was once called the ether field and Stephen Hawking termed "the Mind of God" is now widely recognized in the scientific world as electromagnetic waves, a great energy net that connects all things in the universe from the tiniest parts of the atom to the farthest star. What once was thought to be empty space between things on earth and heavenly bodies, we now know is not empty at all. Everything that exists is connected through this electromagnetic field, this Divine Matrix, or Universal Consciousness. No matter what name you apply to it, science has detected, photographed, and experimented with it and the results are astounding.

Our ancient ancestors wrote about this phenomenon two millennia ago and more. The problem is that we no longer know how to interpret what they wrote. We make the mistake of taking literally what is meant to be symbolic or figurative and take figuratively what is meant to be literal. Why is it that we have no problem with a talking snake in the Garden of Eden but then dismiss the idea that God is physically present inside everything? David, the musician and warrior-king who was called "a man after God's own heart" expressed the omnipresence of God in Psalms 139:

> [7] Where can I go from your Spirit?
>   Where can I flee from your presence?
> [8] If I go up to the heavens, you are there;
>   if I make my bed in the depths, you are there.
> [9] If I rise on the wings of the dawn,
>   if I settle on the far side of the sea,
> [10] even there your hand will guide me,
>   your right hand will hold me fast.
> [11] If I say, "Surely the darkness will hide me
>   and the light become night around me,"
> [12] even the darkness will not be dark to you;
>   the night will shine like the day,
>   for darkness is as light to you. (NIV)

The Apostle Paul stated in Acts 17:28, *For in him we live and move and have our being.*

Jesus also spoke of everything in creation being connected in the Gospel of Mary.[2] *"Will matter be utterly destroyed or not?"* The Savior

---

[2] The Gospel of Mary (Magdalene) was believed to be written by first century followers of Jesus who listened to Mary teach and wrote down what she said. It is the only Gospel attributed to a woman. Three fragmented copies were found in Nag Hammadi Egypt, two written in Greek and the most complete manuscript in Coptic. Like the book of Thomas, the Gospel of Mary was not selected by the Council of Nicaea for inclusion in the Bible.

replied, *"Every nature, every modeled form, every creature exists in and with each other. They will dissolve again into their proper root. For the nature of matter is dissolved into what belongs to its nature. Whoever has ears to hear should hear."* (7:2-5)

God is everywhere, but not in some otherworldly, mysterious way. He is not like an eavesdropping cloud positioned around the earth so he can see and hear what we are up to, ready to give us a pat on the back or slap on the wrist. *Deus* is literally, physically everywhere, from the atoms that make up the cells of our bodies to the furthest star astronomers have yet discovered. He created everything that is, and it all rests inside of Him. Also discovered in Nag Hammadi were two manuscripts of the Gospel of Truth, one in Greek and one in Coptic. Most scholars believe the Council of Nicaea chose to omit this treatise from the canonized Bible because they did not understand it, therefore how could lesser educated men? It includes many references to this very fact, an understanding that was lost to Western civilization for two thousand years. *All have sought for the one from whom they have come forth. All have been within him, the illimitable, the inconceivable, who is beyond all things.* A few verses later: *He is the one who set the All in order and the All is within him.* God is in everything, and everything is in Him. When we smell a flower, touch a snowflake, or stroke our pet, we are experiencing an expression of God. He plainly is the air we breathe, the food we eat, the space we occupy. When we hug our loved one we are hugging God. Likewise, when we strike out in anger and hit another, or yell obscenities at a bad driver - that is God, too.

The poetically cryptic verses that open the Book of John are familiar to Christian church-goers:

> 1 In the beginning was the Word, and the Word was with God, and the Word was God. ² He was with God in the beginning. ³ Through him all things were made; without him nothing was made that has been made. ⁴ In him was life, and that life was the light of all mankind. ⁵ The light shines in the darkness, and the darkness has not overcome (or comprehended) it. (John 1:1-5, NIV)

I John 1:5 makes the same concept clearer - *This is the message we have heard from him and declare to you: God is light; in him there is no darkness at all.* (NIV)

We can now consider these texts in the context of what we know through science. God is not metaphorically light, but rather waves of electromagnetic energy comprised of tiny photons. He is literally made of light! Everything in the universe is comprised of these photons and everything in the universe is connected through the quantum field of the Divine Matrix, the conscious Mind of God. Whether we are aware of it or not, we are never truly alone because God lives inside us holding the atoms of our bodies together. If He were to stop, for only an instant, we would disintegrate into a billion microscopic particles and cease to be in a physical form. So God not only initiated his design with the "big bang" of his omnipotent voice booming out into the void to begin the chain reaction of creation; every day He sustains our essence, our physical and spiritual being, essentially giving us life.

Perhaps you have heard of the Space-Time Continuum. It was proposed by Albert Einstein and is widely accepted today. According to the Special Theory of Relativity, time and space are integrally connected; the universe thus exists not in three dimensions, but four, the fourth being time. We have long been familiar with the concept that God is infinite in time, that He had no beginning and has no end, the Alpha and Omega, and that He has always been and will always be. Science is simply another language through which God communicates with us, another way to reveal Himself to His creation. He made us intelligent, and He made us curious so that we would look for Him in many ways. If Einstein was correct—and the best of contemporary science says that he was—then time and space are connected. So for God to be infinite in time, it would logically follow that He must also be infinite in space.

Let's take a moment to comprehend the concept just presented to you. God is infinite in time and space. So, how big is God? He is in all things, connects all things, and contains all things. He encompasses the entire universe within His being. How big is that? Infinitely large. As astronomers and cosmologists develop better telescopes and instruments with which to document space, more and more galaxies are being discovered all the time.

Every time they look, they see more. That leaves only two viable theories: the universe is constantly expanding, or the universe is infinite in size. So either when God began creation eons upon eons ago, when He spoke those immortal words, "Let there be light," the creation process continues to reverberate through the cosmos without cessation, or the universe simply has no end.

This concept of God is not limited to Judeao-Christian-Islamic traditions. The Hindu faith has a markedly similar concept of the Supreme Being. *"Parambrahma (Spirit or God) is everlasting, complete, without beginning or end. It is one, indivisible Being."* (Swami Sri Yukteswar, The Holy Science, Sutra 1) *"The Eternal Father, God, Swami Parambrahma, is the only Real Substance and is all in all in the universe."* (Swami Sri Yukteswar, The Holy Science, Sutra 1) While Buddhism doesn't acknowledge the person of God, it strongly promotes the same concepts. "All phenomena, link together in a mutually conditioning network." (Buddha) *The impermanence and interdependence of all things, that everything is in constant flux is of profound importance to Buddhist philosophy. The metaphysics of space and motion is very Buddhist in its foundations for it agrees that everything is interconnected and in a perpetual state of change. One thing (space) exists and contains within it the wave motion of space which is the second thing that can exist within the one thing. This motion is a wave motion so we are simply saying that space is vibrating, that space is a wave medium and has waves flowing through it. Thus the 'Changing / Flux' can now be related to the 'Unchanging / Eternal' as the motion of waves (changing) exists in an infinite and eternal space.* (http://www.spaceandmotion.com/Philosophy-Hinduism-Hindu.htm)

Tao, or Dao, in ancient Chinese dates back to the sixth century B.C. and a book credited to philosopher Laozi called *Tao de Ching.* Tao exactly translates as "The Way," but has a description similar to Parambrahma, the Divine Matrix, and God. The philosopher observed there is a supernatural origin which guides everything that occurs across the galaxy, the earth, and human beings. He called it "Tao", a force which existed before time, and even before the universe was created. It is the origin of the world and it thereafter nurtures all the creatures and beings. Its quintessence is the foundation of all nature. Since it is unchangeable and does not evolve with time, it is the ultimate truth. Simply put, Tao is everything.

We have all heard or seen an image of God's hands holding the earth; "He's got the whole world in His hands." That may have even seemed big to us as children. But God is not an old man sitting on a cloud. Neither is He a mystic presence hovering around planet earth. He is much grander, much more overwhelming–He is everywhere in time and space for infinity.

While hopefully some readers will be awed and amazed and some will have their own feelings on the matter confirmed, I suspect others are complaining, "Oh, no! This does not line up with what I believe. Only members of my group, those who believe as I do, who have said the right words and taken the prescribed actions are host to the Spirit of the Living God. *Those* people who live over there, and *those* people who don't adhere to my religion, and *those* people whose lifestyle is clearly wrong aren't in the same category as me. The Spirit of God, His Holy Presence is reserved for the select chosen few–not *everybody!"* Certainly each person has the right to believe whatever they wish; they are also free to miss out on impartation of knowledge, wisdom, and blessings their small cup cannot contain. Jesus said, "Then ye shall know the truth, and the truth shall set you free." (John 8:32) The truth is this: there is no *us* and *them.* There is only one human race, only *us.* All human beings are the sons and daughters of the Living God, all beloved by the Father and created in His image. Jesus said, "For God so loved *the world"* (John 3:16), not "the Jews" or "the Christians" or "our select few", but the whole world and everyone in it. To miss that is to miss the central theme of the Gospel.

While it is true that those who seek God have a much greater chance of experiencing fellowship with the Almighty in a more profound way than those who do not, that is not the issue at point. The Catholic Church has long held to the doctrine that the spark of the divine is in every human being on earth waiting to be discovered. The divine spark is the idea, most common to Gnosticism but also present in other Western mystical traditions, that each human being contains within himself a portion of God. Even ancient Greek and Roman philosophers wrote convincingly that human beings hold within them the light of eternity, a destiny beyond this life, a supernatural mark, and an exalted identity. Now science has proven that to be fact. Not all people know God, but God knows all people and extends His infinite Love toward them all. Here is a very powerful, enriching, freeing precept for those who would embrace the truth: 1) God loves me just as much as He loves every other person in the world. 2) God loves every other person in the world just as much as He loves me.

"Okay, *maybe* I can accept that God lives inside all people, but you are trying to tell me he lives in rocks, trees, rivers, animals, asteroids, and comets? Dirt? I burn wood in my fire and eat meat. Am I supposed to change my whole lifestyle?" Don't be confused. Using resources God gave us to use does not hurt or harm Him in any way. The Bible instructs us to give thanks for our food and all things God has provided for us to use; it doesn't say we can't use them. Perhaps you recall the words to a popular Disney song "Colors of the Wind" from the movie *Pocahontas*. The movie was fiction, but the beliefs behind the words of the song are not.

> You think you own whatever land you land on
>
> The Earth is just a dead thing you can claim
>
> But I know every rock and tree and creature
>
> Has a life, has a spirit, has a name
>
> You think the only people who are people
>
> Are the people who look and think like you
>
> But if you walk the footsteps of a stranger
>
> You'll learn things you never knew, you never knew.
>
> (Stephen Schwartz)

Native Americans were correct; the earth is not a dead thing, and every rock, tree, and creature does have a spirit. The Bible tells us this in numerous passages. [11] *Let the heavens rejoice, and let the earth be glad; let the sea roar, and the fullness thereof.* [12] *Let the field be joyful, and all that is therein; then shall all the trees of the wood rejoice*[13] *before the Lord. For He cometh, for He cometh to judge the earth; He shall judge the world with righteousness, and the people with His truth.* (Psalms 96:11-13) [12] *"For ye shall go out with joy, and be led forth with peace; the mountains and the hills shall break forth before you into singing, and all the trees of the field shall clap their hands."* (God speaking in Isaiah 55:12) Then again don't forget the words of Jesus on Palm Sunday when the multitudes called "Hosanna" during His triumphant entry into Jerusalem: *[39] Some of the Pharisees in the crowd said to Jesus, "Teacher, rebuke your disciples!" [40] "I tell you," he replied, "if they keep quiet, the stones will cry out."* (Luke 19:39-40, NIV) *"The seven heavens and the earth and all who dwell in them give glory to Him. There is not a single thing that is not chanting His praise yet you cannot understand their praise. He is ever forbearing, forgiving"* (Quran, 17:44).

I reiterate that one of our most serious problems with interpreting scriptures and holy texts is that we are so constrained by our limited understanding of the universe that we insist "this passage is not to be taken literally." Of course it is! Just because we can't hear it doesn't mean that nature is not praising God. We must look back to Genesis to the very first commandment God issued to mankind in order to find the problem and the solution. Genesis 1:26-27 uses the term "take dominion" in the King James Version and many more modern versions use the term "rule", but both of those words have the wrong connotation. When we think of dominion or ruling, we think of doing and getting anything we want. *"I, great and mighty human, am in charge!"* But when we read the whole Bible, we see that's not exactly what God meant. A modern translation called "The Voice" gives us a much better idea of those verses' intent:

> God: 26 Now let Us conceive a new creation—humanity—made in Our image, fashioned according to Our likeness. And let Us grant them authority over all the earth—the fish in the sea and the birds in the sky, the domesticated animals and the small creeping creatures on the earth.
>
> 27 So God did just that. He created humanity in His image, created them male and female. 28 Then God blessed them and gave them this directive: "Be fruitful and multiply. Populate the earth. I make you trustees of My estate, so care for My creation and rule over the

fish of the sea, the birds of the sky, and every creature that roams across the earth." (Scripture taken from The Voice™. Copyright © 2008 by Ecclesia Bible Society. Used by permission. All rights reserved.)

We will address the reference to "Our image" in a later chapter, but for now let us focus on God's purpose for our relationship with the rest of creation. The elements of nature are given to us to use, but not to abuse. *The earth is the Lord's, and everything in it, the world, and all who live in it;* (Psalms 24:1, NIV) We are commanded to be good stewards over God's earth, to use but also protect the trees, soil, animals, water, and air that we all depend upon. As a species, we have obeyed the "be fruitful and multiply" to the extent we are on the verge of overpopulating the planet. Sadly we have fallen far short of God's directive for being a good trustee of His estate. Do we think God will wave a magic wand and clean up the mess we've made? He has given us powerful intellect and the ability to do it ourselves; the only thing lacking is our will to obey Him. If we truly understand that God inhabits the ocean we have filled with plastic, the sky we have dirtied with smoke, the earth we have littered with our trash, and the rainforests we wantonly destroy, then *maybe* we will realize that *everything* is holy, and *maybe* we will be convicted in our spirits and change our ways.

"But I thought God lived in heaven," some will say. "Doesn't the Bible say God lives in heaven?" This confusion causes many people to think God resides in a faraway place, up in the sky, not near to them. Biblical references to "heaven" have different meanings which often causes the confusion. There is one reference, which comprises about half of the times heaven is mentioned in the Bible, to "the heavens," or "heaven" as meaning space, or the "heavenly bodies." For example: *In the beginning God created the heavens and the earth.* (Genesis 1:1) This reference, and many others, clearly indicate sun, moon, and stars. The other meaning for heaven represents the spiritual realm of El Shaddai, of the kingdom of God. *From that time on Jesus began to preach, "Repent, for the kingdom of heaven has come near."* (Matthew 4:17, NIV)

So in this second usage of the term, we must ask, "What and where is heaven?" The dictionary defines heaven as: "a place regarded in various religions as the abode of God (or the gods) and the angels, and of the good after death, often traditionally depicted as being above the sky." There are various names for heaven including the Elysian Fields of Greek mythology, the Celtic Otherworld, Vaikuntha the highest of heavens in Hinduism, the Fields of Aaru in Egyptian Mythology, Valhalla in Norse mythology, Gan Eden of Judaism, Mictlan of the Aztec people, and many others. What is noteworthy here is that as long as there have been human civilizations, we have believed in an afterlife, a place for that afterlife, and have given it names. Nirvana of the Buddhist tradition is a bit different. It does not designate a place, per se, but rather a state of being, that of perfect peace. That, too, describes heaven.

References to heaven in the Christian Bible vary widely depending on the passage and lead us to the conclusion that heaven is a spiritual realm both separate from and coexisting with our physical realm. Jesus relates a number of parables attempting to explain to us what heaven is like. Other passages describe heaven as a beautiful place full of music with no crying, sickness, or death. But Jesus also tells us that heaven is not just a place you go to when you die, but that it is here and now for those who will embrace it. *[20] Once, on being asked by the Pharisees when the kingdom of God would come, Jesus replied, "The coming of the kingdom of God is not something that can be observed, [21] nor will people say, 'Here it is,' or 'There it is,' because the kingdom of God is in your midst (or is within you)."* (Luke 17:20-21, NIV) From the book of Thomas 1:3: *Jesus said, "If your leaders say to you, 'Look, the (Father's) kingdom is in the sky,' then the birds of the sky will precede you. If they say to you, 'It is in the sea,' then the fish will precede you. Rather, the (Father's) kingdom is within you and it is outside you."*

What is heaven? A spiritual realm of existence that like God had no beginning, has no end, but has always and always will exist. Where is heaven? It is everywhere. It is up in the sky and down in the sea and within the hearts of men. You can experience "heaven on earth" as well as embark on a new adventure after leaving the confines of your mortal body. Understand, when I use the phrase "heaven on earth" I do not mean a condition in which you have the perfect spouse, the best job, a terrific house, excellent health, and nothing bad ever happens to you. I mean when you arrive at the point in your walk with God where your circumstances no longer dictate your feelings and emotions. When Jesus taught the Lord's Prayer, He said "Thy Kingdom come, Thy will be done on earth as it is in heaven." That was in fact His intent for every human being—for the Kingdom of God to be manifest in our hearts. Do you think Jesus would ask us to pray for something unattainable, or that He knew wouldn't be answered for thousands of years? Did He ask His disciples to pray for something He knew they would not be granted? No. We have misinterpreted by thinking we should be praying for the end of the world so God's Kingdom could finally be established, when in reality God's Kingdom was established eons before our world!

Many who have come before us have experienced heaven on earth and we can too when our understanding has become like that of Paul and Silas. Acts chapter 16 tells the story. They were arrested for helping a woman, beaten and whipped, then shackled in the lowest chamber of the local dungeon. But instead of acting as human nature would dictate with anxiety, fear, anger, dismay, and hopelessness, they understood the reality that this was a temporary state. They were free. They didn't have to be controlled by their situation. So what they did do was to sing praises to God. When we are able to create the feelings of peace, love, and joy within our own hearts regardless of our circumstances, then we are experiencing heaven on earth.

Heaven is not just some distant destination that we hope to reach someday; it is within our own beings, sustaining us with life, providing a pathway of communication with the Great Spirit, God our Father, Mother, Creator, and Guide. It is the unseen electromagnetic waves through which the feelings and meditations of our hearts flow into the consciousness of the Almighty, and through which He responds to our souls.

We've discussed names for God, aspects of His spiritual, gender-neutral state, and where to find Him, but still the question remains, "Who is God?" Perhaps the most direct answer can be found in John 4:16. *[16] And so we know and rely on the love God has for us. God is love. Whoever lives in love lives in God, and God in them.*(NIV) Again in 1 John 4:8—*Whoever does not love does not know God, because God is love.*(NIV) Deuteronomy 7:9 gives us a similar definition of God: *Know therefore that the Lord your God is God; he is the faithful God, keeping his covenant of love to a thousand generations of those who love him and keep his commandments.*(NIV) That's who He is; God is love.

In his search for knowledge and wisdom, Gregg Braden visited monasteries and Holy sites around the world to read ancient texts and speak with the monks who preserved those teachings from our ancestors. While in Tibet he had a profound exchange with the old abbot of a Buddhist monastery. Here is how he recounts that conversation:

> Gregg Braden: In the monasteries in Tibet, for example, they say that feeling is the most powerful force in the universe. At one monastery, I asked the abbot, "In your tradition, what is the force that connects everything in the universe?" He answered with a single word. I thought it was a mistranslation, so I asked our translator to ask him again, and he came back with that same word: "Compassion."
>
> I said, "Wait a minute. Is compassion a force of nature that connects everything in the universe—or is it an experience that we have in our hearts?" After the translator had made sure he understood exactly what I'd asked, he answered again with one word: "Yes."

Compassion. It is a feeling, but it is also a force, the very force, or field, or matrix that comprises, contains, and connects all things. It is God. It is even how God describes Himself. Exodus chapter 34 tells about when Moses went back onto the mountain to receive the Ten Commandments for a second time, because he had broken the first set of stone tablets: *⁶ And he passed in front of Moses, proclaiming, "The LORD, the LORD, the compassionate and gracious God, slow to anger, abounding in love and faithfulness, maintaining love to thousands, and forgiving wickedness, rebellion and sin."* (NIV)

Nehemiah reflects the same characteristics: *But you are a forgiving God, gracious and compassionate, slow to anger and abounding in love.* (Nehemiah 9:17, NIV) The Psalms reiterate these same words in many chapters, including Psalm 116:5—*The Lord is gracious and righteous; our God is full of compassion.* Again we see: *How precious, O God, is your constant love! We find protection under the shadow of your wings.* (Palms 36:7, NIV) In fact, the character of the Great and Holy Spirit is so intertwined with love and compassion that I will go so far as to assert that the most egregious blasphemy that can be committed by man is to claim his feelings, words, and actions of hatred in the name of God.

Romans 8:38-39 are two of the most memorized verses in scripture, and for good reason. Let us consider them in light of what we have discovered. *38 For I am convinced that neither death nor life, neither angels nor demons, neither the present nor the future, nor any powers, 39 neither height nor depth, nor anything else in all creation, will be able to separate us from the love of God that is in Christ Jesus our Lord.* (NIV) Paul is trying to explain to people with no knowledge of modern science but who do have the foundation of Greek philosophy that God is everywhere all the time, however not in some vague mystical way. Factually there is no way to physically separate human beings from God because His ethereal essence is contained in tiny bits of light that comprise the building blocks of our bodies and all matter in creation. And we cannot possibly be separated from God's love because God *is* love and that love, that compassion, is what holds the universe in place.

"But if God is so loving and compassionate, why are there so many tragedies in the world? Why is there pain and suffering and evil? Why do bad things happen to good people?" These are questions very often asked and struggled with, so they deserve attention.

There are two basic categories of suffering–natural and man-made. Jesus explains in Matthew 5:45, *"He causes his sun to rise on the evil and the good, and sends rain on the righteous and the unrighteous."* (NIV) Natural disasters happen because of the laws under which the earth was designed to operate. We think of earthquakes and volcanic eruptions which kill large numbers of people at once. But geologists explain that in the big picture, these local tragedies actually prevent the destruction of the whole planet. Think of earth as a giant pressure cooker: the metal outside of the pot with its sealed lid represents the earth's crust and the boiling water inside represents the hot, molten magma that moves within the mantle creating a warm enough environment to support life as we know it. The valve on top of the lid where the steam spits out is like a volcano or fault line. When pressure builds up in the pot, steam escapes through the valve; if it didn't, the pot would explode. The same is true of our planet. Pressure build-ups beneath the crust are released through volcanic and seismic activity. So really what can seem terrible to us actually saves Earth from self-destructing. People today know where the volcanoes and fault lines are; they aren't active all the time but those who choose to live in these areas know the potential exists. God doesn't wake up in the morning and decide He wants to destroy a particular city because He is displeased with it–the geology of the planet is simply a technical force put in place by our Creator.

Hurricanes are another example of a way the planet regulates temperature. When ocean waters get too hot, tropical storms and hurricanes syphon off some of that heat into the energy of the storm. I know many devout believers in the Jehovah described in the Old Testament insist that God is punishing some city by sending the hurricane there; on the contrary. While forces of nature dictate where the storm will land, God provides opportunities for people to exercise compassion, thus fulfilling their reason to exist. Floods, tornadoes, sink holes, wildfires (not started by humans), and a host of other natural disasters are simply the effects of weather, climate, and geology; they present challenges to the populations affected by them, as well as opportunities, but they are not the result of the wrath of an angry god.

Many times people who struggle with the bad things that happen in this world simply aren't looking at the big picture. Humans are a hybrid being, a spiritual force contained in a body of flesh. Both halves require nourishment, exercise, and caring for. One day we will all lose the physical part of ourselves; *There is a time for everything, and a season for every activity under the heavens: ² a time to be born and a time to die.* (Eccl. 3:1-2, NIV) But the spiritual essence of our being continues on for eternity with God in another dimension of the space-time continuum. Our time on this earth is not all there is; it is merely a drop in the bucket, a twinkling of the eye in the face of eternity. Why do some people live to a hundred and others die the day they are born? We simply do not have all the answers to all the questions ever asked. And there are many documented cases of miracles where some power or force did intervene because it was not someone's time to die. But if we believe in a loving God, while we may be sad at our own loss, we need not cry for the one who leaves his flesh behind to move into immortality.

Okay, natural disasters are one thing, but what about all the evils in the world–poverty, war, disease? I know you'll bring up free will, but can't God do something? Yes, I will bring up free will. People chose to be kind or cruel, generous or selfish, and sometimes in making those decisions harm or kill others. By the same token, some people chose to help those in need. God wants us to be His hands and feet in the world, to share His love and compassion with those who are hurting, sick, or destitute. Why aren't we solving the problem of world hunger? We have the ability to do so. Why aren't we creating peace in our world through our own feelings, words, and actions? That, too, is within our grasp. But often we live in misery and prisons of our own making. How we perceive ourselves and the world around us has a huge impact on our lives. In the Gospel of Thomas, second half of verse 3, Jesus says, *"When you know yourselves, then you will be known, and you will understand that you are children of the living Father. But if you do not know yourselves, then you live in poverty, and you are the poverty."* When we understand that we are the masterpieces of God's creation, His beloved children, that we are never alone, never separated from the One who made us, then we comprehend that our riches do not lie in gold or money but in who we actually are and the immortality God has designed for us. If we try to muddle through life thinking we are insignificant dust or that "the one who dies with the most toys wins," then we are poor indeed.

In the Gospel of Mary Jesus taught, *"This is why you get sick and die: because you love what deceives you. Anyone who thinks should consider these matters."* There are bacteria and viruses all over our planet; some are helpful, some benign, and others harmful. Accidents and injuries happen. I am not in any way trying to say as some that it is a person's own fault they have health problems; only the self-righteous say that! But we can do things to participate in our own well-being. There are six parameters of self that need to be in balance to achieve good health: nutrient, movement, breath, thought, feeling, and emotion. Physicians and health specialists are always promoting good nutrition, exercise and to stop smoking as recipes for better health, and some even advise a change of attitude, getting more rest, or minimizing stress as well. We will discuss the significance of thought, feeling, and emotion later on, but for now I will offer you this–what we think about all day long becomes our reality. Aside from obvious delusions, we are who we believe ourselves to be.

Bad things happen sometimes because of the natural order of the world in which we live, sometimes because of wrong actions taken by other humans, and sometimes we bring them upon ourselves through our own ignorance, recklessness, and fears, but God does not smite people because he is mad at them. That is a wrong interpretation of the Bible relying on Old Testament authors' understanding of events, not upon the teachings of Jesus and New Testament revelations. It is also foolish to try to discount or battle with science, because God created science, too. The laws of motion, gravity, genetics, and all the rest were established by Him as parameters in which our universe could operate in an orderly fashion. Occasionally God works in His own unique way to circumvent those laws to achieve a desired outcome, such as the parting of the Red Sea for Moses or the resurrection of Jesus. But true science does not conflict with faith or spirituality in any real way. The problem does not lie with science or with scriptures, rather in our own inability to accurately interpret both. We must also understand that while we live in a material world, we are at our essence spiritual beings, and know that this world is but a flicker in the span of eternity.

"Then why is God such a narcissist, demanding that people worship Him all the time? That doesn't seem right to me." When I hear that complaint, I just smile and shake my head. The fact is that God does not need our praise or worship or prayers or acts of sacrifice or anything else we do; He was around for an eternity before creating humans and He will outlast this universe, and the next, and the one after that. But in truth, we have been given the instruction to praise, thank, and worship for *our* benefit! I promise detailed spiritual and scientific explanations as to why that is so in a later chapter, but I will presage this phenomenal discovery by saying it has everything to do with the human heart.

No, we do not have a vengeful, petty God, nor an egotistical one. He is not small, ineffectual, or indifferent to pain and suffering. Love and compassion without end, composed of pure light, filling the endlessness of space while holding it inside His being, connecting all people, nature, and the farthest reaches of the galaxies, holding the very atoms together, neither male nor female but a complete entity who is infinite in time and space, ever present everywhere, and powerful beyond imagining: I Am, Allah, Yahweh, Jehovah, El Shaddai, Elohim, Divine Matrix, All Mighty, Abba, All Glorious, Baha, Great Spirit, Supreme Being, Universal Consciousness, Tao, Parambrahma, God–from everlasting to everlasting, above all, in all and through all, Amen!

WHO IS JESUS?

27 Jesus and his disciples went on to the villages around Caesarea Philippi. On the way he asked them, "Who do people say I am?"

28 They replied, "Some say John the Baptist; others say Elijah; and still others, one of the prophets."

29 "But what about you?" he asked. "Who do you say I am?"

Peter answered, "You are the Messiah." (Mark 8:27-29, NIV)

Nearly all modern scholars agree that historically the man known as Jesus lived where and when the Bible indicates. Some people say he was a great teacher of love and peace while others assert he was anointed by God though not equal to God. Most Christians proclaim him to be the Son of God, a third of the Holy Trinity (Father, Son, and Holy Spirit). He is mentioned in non-Christian texts and records as well as the New Testament of the Bible. The Quran references Jesus over 90 times. In Islam he is considered God's most important prophet (aside from Mohammed) and is called Christ. Muslims believe Jesus was born of a virgin, lived a sinless life, performed miracles, and brought the Gospel to the people of Israel but was not the Son of God. Dismissing the notion of a "Trinity", they hold to the declaration of Deuteronomy 6:4 *"Hear, O Israel: The Lord our God is one Lord."* The Talmud includes several conflicting accounts of Jesus, all of which deny that he was the promised Messiah.

At this point it is important to examine just what is meant by the term "Messiah." The dictionary gives us: *the promised and expected deliverer of the Jewish people; any expected deliverer; a zealous leader of some cause or project; an exceptional or hoped for liberator of a country or people; Jesus Christ when regarded in this role.* The origin of the word sheds more light on its ultimate meaning: *c.1300, Messias, from Late Latin Messias, from Greek Messias, from Aramaic meshiha and Hebrew mashiah "the anointed" (of the Lord), from mashah "anoint." This is the word rendered in Septuagint as Greek Khristos (*<u>Christ</u>*). In Old Testament prophetic writing, it was used of an expected deliverer of the Jewish nation. The modern English form represents an attempt to make the word look more Hebrew, and dates from the Geneva Bible (1560). Transferred sense of "an expected liberator or savior of a captive people" is attested from 1660s.*

So to be Messiah one must be both anointed (consecrated or made sacred) and a liberator or deliverer. But liberate and deliver from what? At the time of Jesus's life and ministry Israel was a province of Rome, under the authority of the huge, powerful, and pagan empire. Many of his followers believed that he was the Messiah and that he was sent by God to deliver them from the rule of the Romans, granting them their independence once again. They thought he would assume the throne of Israel and be their earthly king. Jesus himself told the people this was not the case.

Christians believe that Jesus was sent by God to deliver them from sin. In Matthew 1:21 an angel tells Joseph, *"She will give birth to a son, and you are to give him the name Jesus, because he will save his people from their sins."* (NIV) Matthew 9 gives the account of Jesus healing a crippled man in which Jesus himself declares he has the authority to forgive sins. *"5 Which is easier: to say, 'Your sins are forgiven,' or to say, 'Get up and walk'? 6 But I want you to know that the Son of Man has authority on earth to forgive sins." So he said to the paralyzed man, "Get up, take your mat and go home." 7 Then the man got up and went home.* (NIV)

What may surprise some readers is the fact that Jesus did not establish a new religion, nor did he ever state that intention. He frequently told people to offer thanks, praise, and worship to God the Father, but never instructed anyone to worship him. At first, The Way was simply an off-shoot of Judaism, until the Jewish high council declared the belief heresy and worked to stamp it out. Followers of Jesus were first called Christians, meaning "little Christs" or "Christ-like" by citizens of Antioch because members of the congregation there were so generous and loving toward everyone. But nowhere in scriptures or any discovered texts did Jesus declare a new religion or ask people to worship him. That was done by followers after his death.

So far we have established that Jesus was a Jewish man who lived in Palestine in the first part of the first century A.D. or C.E. (Common Era). Peter, one of his disciples, declared him to be the Messiah, the anointed one promised in Old Testament prophecies who would come to deliver the Jews, and that what he actually came to deliver them from was not the Roman government, but sin. He was reportedly conceived by the Holy Spirit, born of the Virgin Mary, performed miracles, and rose from the dead three days after his crucifixion, but did not himself start a new religion. Before we move to the next step in examining who Jesus is, we need to stop and answer the question, what is sin? That is supposed to be what he came to save us from, right?

How do we define sin? Dictionary definitions include: *transgression of divine law; any reprehensible or regrettable action, behavior, lapse, etc.; great fault or offense.* Many people would say breaking one of the Ten Commandments or quote Dante's "Seven Deadly Sins" from *The Inferno.* Romans 3:23 states, *"For all have sinned and fall short of the glory of God."* Some Christian pastors say that sin is disobeying God or God's law or God's word. Billy Graham was quoted as saying, "A sin is any thought or action that falls short of God's will. God is perfect, and anything we do that falls short of His perfection is sin." While these are all fine answers, I wish to point out an important distinction between "perfection" and "sinlessness." The Bible tells us in Hebrews 4:15 that Jesus was without sin. *For we do not have a high priest who is unable to empathize with our weaknesses, but we have one who has been tempted in every way, just as we*

25

are—yet he did not sin. (NIV) Perfection means to have no flaw, never make a mistake, which is a subtle but distinct difference from not sinning. Sin requires intent. I am sure that Jesus sometimes fell down and skinned his knee, spilled the milk, broke a dish, or exhibited other flaws. Perfection would imply that he was perfect at everything; we have no indication that he was skilled in trades other than carpentry. No sacred texts proclaim him to be an outstanding shipbuilder, mason, tailor, musician, or athlete. To be human means to have imperfections; one cannot possibly understand the human condition without having made a social faux pas or had an accident of some nature. This does not equate to sin. Therefore it is slightly inaccurate to say, "Jesus was perfect" while it is correct to say "Jesus was without sin."

Remember the verse from the Gospel of Thomas that began this text? I want to remind you of it because what I am about to reveal will cause many readers to be troubled. *Jesus says: "The one who seeks should not cease seeking until he finds. And when he finds, he will be troubled. And when he is troubled, he will marvel. And he will reign over all."* The Gospel of Thomas, 2:1-4

If you take all the teachings of Jesus, all the writings of the New Testament, and all we know about God it is very plain to see what sin is: whatever is not love, is sin.

To those who say sin is disobedience to God, didn't God command us to love one another? *Do everything in love.* (1 Corinthians 16:14, NIV) *[12] Therefore, as God's chosen people, holy and dearly loved, clothe yourselves with compassion, kindness, humility, gentleness and patience. [13] Bear with each other and forgive one another if any of you has a grievance against someone. Forgive as the Lord forgave you. [14] And over all these virtues put on love, which binds them all together in perfect unity.* (Colossians 3:12-14, NIV) And for the Leviticus quoters out there, *"Do not seek revenge or bear a grudge against anyone among your people, but love your neighbor as yourself. I am the Lord."* (Lev. 19:18, NIV) There are hundreds of verses instructing us to love everyone–our neighbor, the stranger and foreigner, our brothers and sisters, our enemies, and our God. So if you claim sin is disobeying God's word, His word is full of commands to love.

To those who say sin is falling short of glory of God, I ask "What is God's glory?" It is in fact His love, compassion, and unfailing mercy.

That verse in Romans does not refer to God's power as Creator or Ruler of the universe nor does it refer to His infinity in time and space. When in Matthew 5 Jesus says, *"⁴⁸ Be perfect, therefore, as your heavenly Father is perfect,"* (NIV) he is not asking the impossible; why would Jesus give an instruction that he knew none could fulfill? No, we have to look at the context to see that Jesus is talking about love.

> *⁴³ "You have heard that it was said, 'Love your neighbor and hate your enemy.' ⁴⁴ But I tell you, love your enemies and pray for those who persecute you, ⁴⁵ that you may be children of your Father in heaven. He causes his sun to rise on the evil and the good, and sends rain on the righteous and the unrighteous. ⁴⁶ If you love those who love you, what reward will you get? Are not even the tax collectors doing that? ⁴⁷ And if you greet only your own people, what are you doing more than others? Do not even pagans do that? ⁴⁸ Be perfect, therefore, as your heavenly Father is perfect.* (Matt. 5:43-38, NIV)

To those who say sin is something bad that you do, Jesus corrects this misunderstanding in Matthew 5 by pointing to intent. *²¹ "You have heard that it was said to the people long ago, 'You shall not murder, and anyone who murders will be subject to judgment.' ²² But I tell you that anyone who is angry with a brother or sister will be subject to judgment. Again, anyone who says to a brother or sister, 'Raca,' is answerable to the court. And anyone who says, 'You fool!' will be in danger of the fire of hell."* (NIV) And: *²⁷ "You have heard that it was said, 'You shall not commit adultery.' ²⁸ But I tell you that anyone who looks at a woman lustfully has already committed adultery with her in his heart."* (NIV) According to this teaching what you feel in your heart, be it hatred or lust, is just as much sin as acting on those feelings, even if they do not carry the same consequences. Love is the only pure motivation. Whatever is not love is sin.

A Course in Miracles sets forth the principal that everything in our lives is based on one of two things: love or fear. Gregg Braden teaches that the only two underlying emotions are love and fear. When we combine a thought with an emotion we create a feeling, and those feelings direct the course of our lives. For example, we notice a new family moving in next door who is a different race, religion, or ethnicity than we are. When we combine the thought of the strange people with love we create warm, friendly feelings toward them. Maybe we want to lend a hand moving in or welcome them to the neighborhood. Perhaps we are curious and want to talk with them and learn about their culture. We may even bring them a house-warming gift and offer to show them around. But when fear rises up to join with thoughts of strange people, our feelings turn negative. We may feel suspicious; are they criminals or terrorists? Anger may form; they will bring down my property's value! Jealousy could take root; those people are taking our jobs. If the love of money is the root of all evil, then fear is the root of all sin.

How can it be a sin to be afraid? It is human nature, it is normal to have fear! First let me distinguish that I am not referring to the healthy, life-saving fear of a real imminent danger. If you see an out-of-control vehicle barreling toward you, a little shot of adrenaline should get you dashing out of the way. I do not advocate snake handling or taking unnecessary risks because you have "no fear." I am referring to a spirit of fear as opposed to a spirit of love. Love is the nature of God, the nature He put into our spirit-being at creation. But the flesh half of us contains a nature of fear, both conscious and subconscious, and we must unlearn these fears if we ever hope to experience an abundant life. *[18] There is no fear in love. But perfect love drives out fear, because fear has to do with punishment. The one who fears is not made perfect in love.* (1 John 4:18, NIV)

Do you believe sin is disobedience to God? We are commanded over one hundred times in scriptures to "fear not," or "be not afraid". Perhaps the only other instruction that is repeated that many times is to love others. It is amply clear that two of the most important messages the Creator of all wanted us to grasp are to not be afraid, but to love instead.

There are three universal fears that can drive people's lives and being aware of them may help us to examine ourselves and deal with them in a constructive manner. 1) The fear of abandonment. 2) The fear of inadequacy. 3) The fear of everything out there, the dangers that may be.

Many people have an underlying fear of being alone, deserted, or forsaken. This could derive from an incorrect understanding of God. If one thinks of God as in heaven, or out there far away somewhere rather than living inside of him, he may feel like this powerful entity created the world and then left us here to fend for ourselves. This could lead to a fear of abandonment. *A Course in Miracles* states, "A sense of separation from God is the only lack you really need correct." One can read the words of Deuteronomy 31:8, *The Lord himself goes before you and will be with you; he will never leave you nor forsake you. Do not be afraid; do not be discouraged,"* (NIV) or any of the other passages that give the same promise, but unless he truly embraces and believes it, the fear can manifest. Sometimes when one has a parent abandon the family or die, or as an adult loses a spouse or loved one, this fear is given a foothold. A little voice speaks in our head saying, "Everyone will leave you; you are alone." People who fear being left often have difficulty in relationships, subconsciously expecting the loved one to desert her, just waiting for it to happen. It affects our ability to trust others and build meaningful relationships, and if not addressed can become a self-fulfilling prophecy.

The fear of not measuring up, not being good enough, generates everything from low self-esteem to extreme narcissism. Sometimes an improper religious upbringing is at fault. When one is taught he is a worm, he is dust, he is an awful rotten sinner and deserves to be punished, then he may start to believe it. Maybe it was a parent, teacher, sibling, or peer that told her over and over again, "you're stupid, you can't do anything right," and hearing it enough times, she believed it. But self-esteem aside, this is a tremendously destructive fear. A man who is afraid he doesn't measure up will put others down in an effort to make himself appear superior. This gives rise to all kinds of prejudice, racism, and bigotry often with the accompanying hate speech and violence. "I may not be as good as so-in-so, but I'm better than *them*." This fear molds bullies as well as doormats, those who dish out punishment and those who are content to bear it. But it manifests in other ways as well: jealousy and envy toward someone perceived as having more than us, over-competitiveness, being a show-off, becoming a control freak, greediness, and the list goes on. It may be difficult, but it is vital that we cease comparing ourselves to others or some impossible ideal. We must unlearn what the world has taught us and embrace love. When Jesus commanded, "love your neighbor as yourself," it implies that we must first love ourselves.

It is essential to break this cycle of fear! *A Course in Miracles* states:

"You are the work of God, and His work is wholly lovable and wholly loving. This is how a man must think of himself in his heart, because this is what he is." Ephesians 2:10 from The Voice translation tells us: *For we are the product of His hand, heaven's poetry etched on lives, created in the Anointed, Jesus, to accomplish the good works God arranged long ago.* (Scripture taken from The Voice™. Copyright © 2008 by Ecclesia Bible Society. Used by permission. All rights reserved.) And 1 John 3:1, *See what great love the Father has lavished on us, that we should be called children of God! And that is what we are!* (NIV) It is irrational to fear failure because failure is simply a given. Each and every human being fails at some point; we all fall down and make mistakes, but that doesn't mean we can't fulfill our purpose in life. That misstep does not cause God to love us less. We are his masterpieces! When we truly know, deep down in our heart, who we are, we can root out and discard the fears of abandonment and inadequacy.

But the world really is a dangerous place! There are a multitude of things to be afraid of out there; isn't this third one a legitimate fear? The issue at point is not whether or not there is danger in the world, for certainly there is; the point is do we dwell on the dangers and allow fear of them to rule our lives? Do we choose fear or love? For example, a woman reads an article about someone who died from a new strain of flu; what is her immediate response? Love would mate with the thought and create a feeling of compassion toward the victim of the virus and his family members. Fear would incite feelings of anxiety: "What if I catch it or my child? I must buy more antibacterials and stay away from large crowds. Come to think of it, my throat feels a little scratchy. Let me research this new flu on the internet so I can watch out for its symptoms." Sometimes our focus attracts the very things–good or bad–that we focus on. Just because a bug is going around doesn't mean you will get it; however, nervous anxiety actually works in our bodies to lower our immunity to disease, therefore making it more likely we will catch the flu. We will examine this in more detail later on.

Muggers learn how to read potential marks; if they didn't, they wouldn't last long in that profession. Any mugger will tell you they stay away from people who stride confidently across the dark parking lot with their shoulders back projecting an image of strength. They target the nervous, jittery type, hunched in fear looking all around them with wide eyes. Even a small mugger figures he can overpower someone who is already afraid.

There are dangers in the world, but worrying about them will not keep them from happening. Fear of all the bad possibilities actually acts as a magnet to draw those bad things to you. *What I feared has come upon me; what I dreaded has happened to me.* (Job 3:25) Instead of being fearful of everything out there, we should strive to be prepared. Have emergency supplies and a plan in case of a tornado, hurricane, earthquake, flood, or fire. If you know you are prepared, you can be confident instead of afraid. Educate yourself as to what actions to take in various situations so that if that eventuality ever presents itself you will know what to do rather than panic. Ultimately, when we give into worry, anxiety, and fearfulness we are acting out of a lack of trust; we are in essence saying that we don't trust God to take care of us. "But what about this good Christian, Jew, Muslim, Hindu, or Buddhist who was always trusting and something bad still happened to her?" Be assured of this–in the course of your life something bad *will* happen to you! Something bad happens to everyone at one time or another, and if that bad thing results in death remember it is only a transition to another life. *The Lord is my light and my salvation — whom shall I fear? The Lord is the stronghold of my life — of whom shall I be afraid?* (Psalm 27:1, NIV) *A Course in Miracles* teaches us, "When you are afraid of anything, you are acknowledging its power to hurt you. Remember that where your heart is, there is your treasure also. You believe in what you value. If you are afraid, you are valuing wrongly."

[8] *Be alert and of sober mind. Your enemy the devil prowls around like a roaring lion looking for someone to devour.* (1 Peter 5:8, NIV) It would be just as accurate to say, "Watch out! Your enemy, Fear, prowls around like a roaring lion, looking for someone to devour." Fear can devour us, make us impotent, and steal our joy. It can control every aspect of our lives if we allow it to, and the tricky part is that most of the time we don't even realize it is happening. I challenge the reader as I challenge myself to search deep and identify fears that are manipulating us and holding us back from the abundant life our loving God planned for us.

"Is that it? Love or fear?" There is another motivator that could be considered separate from fear - selfishness. Selfishness can be expressed through the twin sins of lust and greed. What is significant to note is that neither selfishness, lust, nor greed can ever be generated from a spirit of love. Therefore, it can be stated that everything we do, say, and feel is either love or not-love. If it is not-love, then it is sin.

"But I certainly feel other emotions; what about those?" As humans we have the capacity to experience a wide range of feelings, all of which are legitimate; when I speak of love here, it is not as one of many possible emotions, but as an underlying force that drives our lives. We typically view emotions as falling into one of two categories–positive and negative. In the third chapter we will go into great detail as to how these emotions affect our bodies, thought process, and spiritual well-being, but for now let's just acknowledge them. Positive emotions are those feelings that make life worth living: joy, happiness, anticipation, excitement, affection, empathy, compassion, contentment, gratitude, appreciation, peace, and the emotion of love.

We want to live in these as much as it is possible, but the negative emotions that sweep over us at times are also valid. People and circumstances may cause us to feel sad, disappointed, frustrated, hurt, vulnerable, lonely, or angry. It is okay to allow these emotions... for a time. Even Jesus was sad sometimes. The Bible records three occasions when he cried, though I am certain there were others: when his friend Lazarus died, when he cried over the people of Jerusalem who did not understand what he tried to teach them, and on the eve of his execution when he knew what was about to transpire. The key is to not wallow in self-pity nor to dwell in negative emotions. *Weeping may stay for the night, but rejoicing comes in the morning.* (Psalms 30:5, NIV) *You turned my wailing into dancing; you removed my sackcloth and clothed me with joy.* (Psalms 30:11, NIV) *26 "In your anger do not sin": Do not let the sun go down while you are still angry, 27 and do not give the devil a foothold.* (Ephesians 4:26-27, NIV) Jesus got angry at the money changers in the Temple for cheating those who had come to worship and cheapening God's house, and again at the Pharisees for misleading the people and being hypocrites. But he never stopped loving the people he was angry with.

Therefore, we should train ourselves to keep our minds and emotions fixed on the positive. *8 Finally, brothers and sisters, whatever is true, whatever is noble, whatever is right, whatever is pure, whatever is lovely, whatever is admirable—if anything is excellent or praiseworthy—think about such things.* (Philippians 4:8, NIV) When we do feel those negative emotions, we should let ourselves cry or be angry to release what could otherwise fester into something destructive, but we should not get caught in their trap. Being angry is not a sin, but anger can devolve into thoughts, feelings, and actions that are not rooted in love. Everyone is sad sometimes, but if we let it consume us we become self-centered on our own pain forgetting about others whom we were created to love. Allow yourself to experience the negative emotion and look deeper to determine its ultimate cause. When someone says something that hurts your feelings, do you feel hurt because you love that person and his words make you feel unloved, or is it because you already live in the fear that you are unlovable and his words confirm that fear? Never allow anything or anyone to steal your joy!

"What about all those sexual sins? If love can never be sin, then what about sex? We are always hearing how bad it is even if everyone always does it anyway." First, we must understand the huge and fundamental difference between lust and love. The Bible does in fact name several sexual sins, all based on the motivation behind the act, not the act itself. God granted humans a very powerful, intimate gift with the sexual experience in which two distinct individuals can be joined together in an outpouring of love. But if love is not the motivating force, the gift of God is cheapened. Prostitution is listed as sexual sin because it is about an exchange of money for services, often between complete strangers with not even a hint of love. Adultery is a sin because it comprises breaking a vow, something God takes seriously. If the parties involved truly loved each other, they would not put each other in the position to break the vow; they would dissolve the first marriage before proceeding into a new relationship. In adultery, where is the love for the actual spouse? Where is the love for God in whose eyes the vow was made? Adultery is inherently a selfish act therefore not motivated by true love.

"What about 'pre-marital sex'?" First of all, the Bible never uses the phrase 'pre-marital sex' nor does it specifically condemn sex between engaged persons. The Bible does use the term 'fornication' which the English dictionary defines as sex between unmarried persons. However, that is not how the word was used in the original Hebrew and Greek. From Strong's Concordance:

2181 zanah zaw-naw' a primitive root (highly-fed and therefore wanton); to commit adultery (usually of the female, and less often of simple fornication, rarely of involuntary ravishment); figuratively, to commit idolatry (the Jewish people being regarded as the spouse of Jehovah):--(cause to) commit fornication, X continually, X great, (be an, play the) harlot, (cause to be, play the) whore, (commit, fall to) whoredom, (cause to) go a-whoring, whorish.

8457 taznuwth taz-nooth' or taznuth {taz-nooth'}; from 2181; harlotry, i.e. (figuratively) idolatry:--fornication, whoredom.

1608. ekporneuo ek-porn-yoo'-o from 1537 and 4203; to be utterly unchaste:--give self over to fornication.

4202. porneia por-ni'-ah from 4203; harlotry (including adultery and incest); figuratively, idolatry:--fornication. 4203. porneuo porn-yoo'-o from 4204; to act the harlot, i.e. (literally) indulge unlawful lust (of either sex), or (figuratively) practise idolatry:--commit (fornication)

Here we see a much fuller, deeper, and darker vision of fornication that has nothing to do with love. The greater implications referred to orgies, particularly as part of pagan rituals and idol worship having nothing to do with feelings of love. It denotes promiscuity, or "casual sex." It is easy to determine the difference: lust is selfish, seeking one's own gratification with little or no regard to his partner. How does it make *me* feel? How do *I* benefit? Whereas love is just the opposite, seeking to please and elevate the other. How can I please *you*? What can I *give*? Therefore, it is safe to say that sex is a beautiful gift when used as an expression of deep bonding between two people who are committed to each other exclusively in love, best–but not solely–within the bonds of marriage. What exactly constitutes marriage in the eyes of God? Is it a legal contract issued by the state or a ceremony performed in a church? Either of these can occur without true love being present. Or is it when two individuals dedicate themselves in love and fidelity to each other, with or without the afore mentioned license or ceremony? Licenses and sacraments are good, but without the corresponding feelings of the heart they are merely convenient lies. I will also add that whatever the individual engages in that makes her feel guilt, whatever he believes to be wrong, is wrong for her or him as long as that belief persists.

Readers of the Bible may have noticed that rape is not listed with other sexual sins, and the reason for that is the same as why law enforcement today consider rape a violent crime, not a sex crime. Rape has very little to do with sex and everything to do with domination over another individual. It is most assuredly a sin because the motivation is never love. While it can be lust, it is usually born out of a fear of inferiority. The rapist has to try to prove his superiority by forcing his will upon another, placing the victim in the subordinate position.

But what about all the ordinary things in life? Is *everything* supposed to be love? Actually, yes. 1 Corinthians 16:14 instructs us, *Do everything in love.* (NIV) Why do you go to work? Is it to make as much money as possible to in impress your peers, because you have to, because you don't want to live in your parents' basement anymore, because your wife will divorce you if you don't? Or is it because you love God and want to do your best at everything you do, because you love your family and want to provide for them, because you love your community and want to contribute in a positive way, or because you love yourself and want to excel and improve? Why do you volunteer for military service? Is it because you want a tough-guy image and respect, because you want to kill people and that's a legal way to do it, because you've been told you aren't skilled, educated, talented, or qualified to do anything else? Or is it because you love your family, your community, and your country and by serving in the military you keep them safer? Why do you clean the house? Is it because you don't want to be embarrassed when people come over, or because you are afraid your husband will be angry if you don't? Or is it out of love for your family and yourself? Is taking the children to school and activities an obligation or a privilege? Going shopping, doing the chores, mowing the grass–EVERYTHING we do is either from a motivation of love or it isn't. And if it isn't born of love, then it doesn't amount to a heap of trash.

Read again the familiar words of 1 Corinthians 13 with the idea of everything being love or not-love, and what is not-love being sin.

> 13 If I speak in the tongues of men or of angels, but do not have love, I am only a resounding gong or a clanging cymbal. ² If I have the gift of prophecy and can fathom all mysteries and all knowledge, and if I have a faith that can move mountains, but do not have love, I am nothing. ³ If I give all I possess to the poor and give over my body to hardship that I may boast, but do not have love, I gain nothing.
>
> ⁴ Love is patient, love is kind. It does not envy, it does not boast, it is not proud. ⁵ It does not dishonor others, it is not self-seeking, it is not easily angered, it keeps no record of wrongs. ⁶ Love does not delight in evil but rejoices with the truth. ⁷ It always protects, always trusts, always hopes, always perseveres.
>
> ⁸ Love never fails. But where there are prophecies, they will cease; where there are tongues, they will be stilled; where there is knowledge, it will pass away. ⁹ For we know in part and we prophesy in part, ¹⁰ but when completeness comes, what is in part disappears. ¹¹ When I was a child, I talked like a child, I thought like a child, I reasoned like a child. When I became a man, I put the ways of childhood behind me. ¹² For now we see only a reflection as in a mirror; then we shall see face to face. Now I know in part; then I shall know fully, even as I am fully known.
>
> ¹³ And now these three remain: faith, hope and love. But the greatest of these is love. (NIV)

Moses gave his people Ten Commandments, words from I AM for the children of earth to use as a guide, but the leaders became legalists, burdening the people with hundreds of laws so that they lost sight of what mattered. Jesus came to hit the reset button and show the sons and daughters of the Most High what the Master of the Universe intended. He only gave us two commandments.

Mark 12:28-31

[28] One of the teachers of the law came and heard them debating. Noticing that Jesus had given them a good answer, he asked him, "Of all the commandments, which is the most important?"

[29] "The most important one," answered Jesus, "is this: 'Hear, O Israel: The Lord our God, the Lord is one. [30] Love the Lord your God with all your heart and with all your soul and with all your mind and with all your strength.' [31] The second is this: 'Love your neighbor as yourself.' There is no commandment greater than these." (NIV)

The Gospel of Mary's version of the "Great Commission," the last instructions of Jesus Christ before he ascended into Heaven, includes slightly different words than the Matthew version. It is very powerful and one might see why church and government representatives at the Council of Nicaea chose to omit them from the canonized Bible. Let these words take root in your heart: "Go then, preach the good news about the kingdom. Do not lay down any rule beyond what I determined for you, nor promulgate law like the lawgiver, or else you might be dominated by it." (8:18-19) Jesus did not approve of the Scribes, Sadducees, Pharisees, and religious law-givers of his day because they had warped God's intent and placed their rules above God's rules. Therefore, Jesus made the rules simple: love God and love your fellow man.

Paul in Romans 10:13 reiterates the principle. *Love does no harm to a neighbor. Therefore love is the fulfillment of the law.* (NIV) Peter echoes the same in 2 Peter 1:5-7 *For the entire law is fulfilled in keeping this one command: "Love your neighbor as yourself."* (NIV) This is the Gospel; this is the Good News that Jesus came to bring us—God loves everyone in the whole world, and all He wants from us is to love Him and love each other.

It is just that simple—and just that hard. "Love that girl with all the tattoos? Love that guy with the hair? Love that mean neighbor, that foreigner, that Muslim, Jew, atheist, that gay or transgender person? Love the idiot who cut me off in traffic? Love my wife, husband, mother, father, child, weird aunt, gross uncle, despicable boss, shiftless employee, griping co-worker, homeless guy with the sign, rich SOB with his billions, *all those people?*" Precisely. John Lennon was right: "All you need is love."

"Now wait just a minute—love is important, but what about right doctrine? We have to believe the correct creeds, teachings, and dogmas." I'm sorry, but whose are the right ones, and who decides? Each religion and denomination says that they are right, when the plain and simple fact is there is no correct doctrine! None of them are "right," and 1 Corinthians 13:9, 10 & 12 clearly says so: *⁹ For we know in part, and we prophesy in part. ¹⁰ But when that which is perfect is come, then that which is in part shall be done away. ¹² For now we see through a glass, darkly; but then face to face: now I know in part; but then shall I know even as also I am known.* (NIV) No one knows everything there is to know about God, no religious group or leader, no book or interpretation, no not one. We each try to glean as much truth as we can to live by, but none of us gets it all right. However on this one truth we can be completely, positively certain—love is always right, and love is never wrong.

Jesus was a real person, identified as the Messiah, or Christ, who came to save us from sin and deliver us into love. Throughout the Bible, he is referred to by different names, each referencing a different aspect of his person or his mission. He is called the Word of God because he brought God's words to man; the Lamb of God because he sacrificed himself for the betterment of humanity; son of David because he was born out of the lineage of King David as God promised. Jesus is also called the Prince of Peace. Isaiah 9:6 gave us this prophecy: *For to us a child is born, to us a son is given, and the government will be on his shoulders. And he will be called Wonderful Counselor, Mighty God, Everlasting Father, Prince of Peace.* Jesus spoke to his disciples about true peace. *"Peace I leave with you; my peace I give you. I do not give to you as the world gives. Do not let your hearts be troubled and do not be afraid."* (John 14:27, NIV) and *"I have told you these things, so that in me you may have peace. In this world you will have trouble.*

But take heart! I have overcome the world." (John 15:33, NIV) The world thinks of peace as the absence of conflict, but the peace Jesus embodied and taught about is much more. It includes peace with our neighbors but also peace with God and peace with ourselves, peace within our hearts. It is not the absence of something negative, but the presence of something positive. The peace spoken of in the above passages implies confidence and courage, freedom from worry and anxiety, an underlying certainty that even if the world is falling down around our ears, everything will be alright. *And the peace of God, which transcends all understanding, will guard your hearts and your minds in Christ Jesus.* (Phil. 4:7, NIV)

Jesus was also called the Son of God, and while not rebuking that denotation, he referred to himself as the "Son of Man." Because he was born of a woman, Mary, who is proclaimed in scriptures to be a virgin, the human mind has concluded that he had to have a father and that father had to be God. While there is nothing wrong with this belief, I am willing to go one step further. My study of sacred texts and lifelong pursuit of spiritual truth leads me to believe that Jesus was actually Emmanuel, God with us, a portion of the Divine miraculously poured into human form to live among us, experience what a mortal life is like, and to more accurately teach us what His purpose and design for humanity has always been. While God continued to hold the molecules of the universe in place, making sure every law of nature and heavenly body continued to function, a part of His essence, His consciousness, took on the form of a seed in Mary's womb, was born a human baby, and grew into a man to fulfill a specific purpose.

We just read in Isaiah 9:6, *For to us a child is born, to us a son is given, and the government will be on his shoulders. And he will be called Wonderful Counselor, Mighty God, Everlasting Father, Prince of Peace.* (NIV) This prophecy includes "Mighty God," and "Everlasting Father" in a list of names for Jesus. Now how can Jesus be his own father unless he and God are one and the same, simply a different aspect or representations of the same being? And why would Isaiah call this child "Mighty God" if he was to be anything less? Isaiah also includes the title "Wonderful Counselor," often a name used to refer to the Holy Spirit, third member of the Trinity. So not only is Jesus the same as God, he is the same as the Holy Spirit; the three are one.

Another passage that supports this belief comes from Acts 9 in the story of Saul's conversion.

> 9 Meanwhile, Saul was still breathing out murderous threats against the Lord's disciples. He went to the high priest [2] and asked him for letters to the synagogues in Damascus, so that if he found any there who belonged to the Way, whether men or women, he might take them as prisoners to Jerusalem. [3] As he neared Damascus on his journey, suddenly a light from heaven flashed around him. [4] He fell to the ground and heard a voice say to him, "Saul, Saul, why do you persecute me?"

> [5] "Who are you, Lord?" Saul asked.

> "I am Jesus, whom you are persecuting," he replied. [6] "Now get up and go into the city, and you will be told what you must do."

> [7] The men traveling with Saul stood there speechless; they heard the sound but did not see anyone. [8] Saul got up from the ground, but when he opened his eyes, he could see nothing. So they led him by the hand into Damascus. [9] For three days he was blind and did not eat or drink anything. (NIV)

It has already been established that God is light, made of pure light, tiny photons that are the smallest known building blocks of atoms. Throughout scriptures God is referred to as light. So if Jesus is also light, a light so brilliant that it knocked Saul down and blinded him for three days, it would logically follow that Jesus and God are the same. Further evidence comes from the words of Jesus in John 8:12 - *When Jesus spoke again to the people, he said, "I am the light of the world. Whoever follows me will never walk in darkness, but will have the light of life."* (NIV)

Another mention in in the opening of the book of John which was referenced earlier.

1 In the beginning was the Word, and the Word was with God, and the Word was God. ² He was with God in the beginning. ³ Through him all things were made; without him nothing was made that has been made. ⁴ In him was life, and that life was the light of all mankind. ⁵ The light shines in the darkness, and the darkness has not overcome it. (NIV)

The implication made is that Jesus was the Word, and the Word was God; therefore, Jesus was also God. It is not that there is more than one God, but rather one God with more than one way to present Himself. God appeared to Moses in a bush that burned but was not consumed. Jesus was God in the form of a human, but God Himself is not human. *¹⁸ No one has ever seen God, but the one and only Son, who is himself God and is in closest relationship with the Father, has made him known.* (John 1:18, NIV) Jesus himself repeated this concept in John 14.

⁷ "If you really know me, you will know my Father as well. From now on, you do know him and have seen him."

⁸ Philip said, "Lord, show us the Father and that will be enough for us."

⁹ Jesus answered: "Don't you know me, Philip, even after I have been among you such a long time? Anyone who has seen me has seen the Father. How can you say, 'Show us the Father'? ¹⁰ Don't you believe that I am in the Father, and that the Father is in me? The words I say to you I do not speak on my own authority. Rather, it is the Father, living in me, who is doing his work. ¹¹ Believe me when I say that I am in the Father and the Father is in me; or at least believe on the evidence of the works themselves." (NIV)

Jesus was a man with extraordinary abilities to heal, walk on water, command storms, raise the dead, and a host of other recorded miracles. He came to save people from sin, and many believe He was the Son of

God or God incarnate. But if we look closely, we will see that the salvation Jesus brought to mankind is multifaceted. It is not simply a "get out of hell free" ticket, but something much, much more for here and now as well as there and then.

I believe that something supernatural occurred on the cross. According to many witnesses, Jesus died, was buried, and then was seen alive by as many as 500 people afterward. His resurrected body, however, was not exactly like the one that died. At first even those closest to him, Mary Magdalene and his disciples, did not recognize him until they heard him speak. The resurrected Jesus could appear and disappear and pass through walls, yet Thomas was able to touch and feel that he was solid. Could he always have done those things had he chosen to? After all, it is the power and presence of God that is the glue making matter solid; if he chooses, he can easily allow what we understand as objects to move through each other. Did Jesus always have that power and simply choose not to use it until then, or did he only receive that astonishing ability after he was resurrected?

No mortal knows precisely what work was done in the spiritual realm when Jesus hung on the cross. People say they know, but they don't; how can we? Who traveled the dimensions with him as a witness? But of this one point I am completely certain—if the mystery of Christ's death and resurrection provided salvation for one person's soul, it provided salvation for every person's soul. The message Jesus brought to earth was that God loves everyone, not just a select few, and if his sacrifice, or journey through dimensions, or whatever you want to call it that transpired over the course of that fateful weekend was powerful enough to save one sinner, then it was powerful enough to save every sinner. This act speaks to eternal salvation, our destiny in the afterlife, which may or may not have ever been in question.

I have been a part of various denominations and attended churches across the board from extremely conservative to very progressive. What I am about to share with you was not taught to me by any of them. At this time I want to share some very well-known passages of the Bible with a fresh interpretation which I believe speaks in a powerful way. I will begin with a phrase from Matthew 6:13, the "Lord's Prayer." *And lead us not into temptation, but deliver us from evil.* The common interpretation of this line is a petition of protection from evil or bad things happening to us, or protection from the devil. I propose that is not what this line means at all, but rather to deliver us from perpetrating evil ourselves. Look at the entirety of the line - *lead us not into temptation*, the thoughts, emotions, and circumstances that would prompt us to sin, and then adds *but deliver us from evil*, the evil that we may think, feel, say, or do. This verse is not about keeping us safe from harm, but keeping us safe from harming someone else, or harming our own soul through the evil of the sin residing within us. What sin? Whatever is not love. It is actually a prayer to protect us from ourselves. Jesus died at the hands of angry religious authorities who didn't want him usurping their power, proselyting their members, telling crowds that they were wrong; so they conspired with the hated Roman government to have him executed. Jesus was not protected from this evil; all the disciples except for John died violent deaths, martyrs to The Way. Neither he nor his followers for several centuries were delivered from violent acts of evil. Would he tell his students to say a prayer that he knew wasn't going to be answered? But when you see this verse in a new light–that the evil we need protection from is not without, but within–then it makes perfect sense.

Of all the verses in the Bible one stands out as exclusive in nature. It is used to pressure people into "conversions", promote the superiority of the Christian religion, and if possible, to bar others from all over the globe from entering the Kingdom of Heaven. They are the words of Jesus in John 14:6. Here is the verse in context:

> 14 "Do not let your hearts be troubled. You believe in God; believe also in me. ² My Father's house has many rooms; if that were not so, would I have told you that I am going there to prepare a place for you? ³ And if I go and prepare a place for you, I will come back and take you to be with me that you also may be where I am. ⁴ You know the way to the place where I am going."
>
> ⁵ Thomas said to him, "Lord, we don't know where you are going, so how can we know the way?"

> **⁶Jesus answered, "I am the way and the truth and the
> life. No one comes to the Father except through me.** ⁷
> If you really know me, you will know my Father as well.
> From now on, you do know him and have seen him."
> (NIV)

For centuries Christians have used this verse to promote the idea that only Christians, self-proclaimed followers of Jesus Christ, will ever see God or know God or spend an eternity with Him in Heaven. That notion when carefully examined in the light of scriptures and what we know about the character of God is ludicrous! They want to claim on the one hand that God is love, that He loves the whole world, and that He is just and righteous, while at the same time declare, "Oh, and by the way, we are the only ones who get to go to Heaven." Think for a moment of all the humans who have ever lived, billions and billions over two hundred thousand years. If God is just and loving, is it likely that only a select few who were fortunate enough to have been born in a country and a family where Christianity was taught and promoted get to go to Heaven and everyone else is just out of luck? What about all the people who lived before the time of Christ? It is preposterous to think that the God of the universe, who is Himself compassion, who is well acquainted with the imperfections of His creation, would condemn or even exclude the bulk of humanity and only favor these few. Additionally, there are scriptures to support a more universal salvation.

Acts 10:1-2 reads, *At Caesarea there was a man named Cornelius, a centurion in what was known as the Italian Regiment. ²He and all his family were devout and God-fearing; he gave generously to those in need and prayed to God regularly.* (NIV) This man was not Jewish nor was he Christian. He was a Roman and yet note what it says about him. He believed there was a God, and he did the things God requires, namely giving generously to those in need and seeking to know his creator through prayer. In the story an angel speaks to him and tells him to send for the Apostle Peter, who eventually comes to realize the Good News is not for Jews alone. God is a rewarder of those who seek Him, regardless of their nationality or religious background.

Another example comes from Acts 8:26-39. There was a certain

Ethiopian eunuch, an important government treasury officer, who had traveled to Jerusalem and was on his way home. Judaism had at that time spread to Ethiopia but was not the dominant religion in the region. The man would have been black, not tan as Jews were, and his native language and style of dress were foreign as well. Yet here he was riding in his chariot reading from Jewish scriptures. God miraculously transported Philip to the spot the eunuch was passing so that he could share the teachings of Jesus with him. God cares about people from every nation of the world, not just yours or mine.

16 And so we know and rely on the love God has for us. God is love. Whoever lives in love lives in God, and God in them. 17 This is how love is made complete among us so that we will have confidence on the day of judgment (1 John 4:16-17, NIV) Whoever lives in love, lives in God, and God in them; therefore, love is what matters most. *Whoever has my commands and keeps them is the one who loves me. The one who loves me will be loved by my Father, and I too will love them and show myself to them.* (1 John 4:11, NIV) What commands? Jesus only gave two–love God and love your neighbor. Again Christ declared in Matthew 7:21, *"Not everyone who says to me, 'Lord, Lord,' will enter the kingdom of heaven, but only the one who does the will of my Father who is in heaven."* (NIV) Therefore even people throughout time and geography who never heard of the Jewish God nor the name of Jesus are considered part of the family if they live a life of love. Not the ones who wear a certain label, say the right words, attend the approved functions, or participate in sacred rituals, but those who do what Jesus said to do–even if they never heard his name–are those who are approved by God.

In fact, this concept is so important to God that He made certain every culture, race, religion, and curve of the globe got the message. Did you think God only spoke to the Hebrew people and simply ignored the rest of the world? Preposterous! There is one God, and He is God of *all*. The Golden Rule is universal and here are its various forms:

> "Ascribe not to any soul that which thou wouldst not have ascribed to thee, and say not that which thou doest not."
> "Blessed is he who preferreth his brother before himself."
> Baha'u'llah (Bahai)

FROM GLORY TO GLORY

"This is the sum of Dharma [duty]: Do naught unto others which would cause you pain if done to you." Mahabharata, 5:1517 (Brahmanism, Hinduism)

"Hurt not others in ways that you yourself would find hurtful," and "One should seek for others the happiness one desires for oneself." (Buddhism)

"Do not do to others what you do not want them to do to you," Doctrine of the Mean, "What I do not wish men to do to me, I also wish not to do to men." Analects 15:23 and "Try your best to treat others as you would wish to be treated yourself, and you will find that this is the shortest way to benevolence." Mencius VII.A.4 (Confucianism)

"Do for one who may do for you, that you may cause him thus to do." The Tale of the Eloquent Peasant (ancient Egyptian)

"Do not to another what you would not yourself experience." Manco Capoc, founder of the empire of Peru

"None of you [truly] believes until he wishes for his brother what he wishes for himself." Number 13 of Imam *"Al-Nawawi's Forty Hadiths."* (Islam)

"In happiness and suffering, in joy and grief, we should regard all creatures as we regard our own self." Lord Mahavira, 24th Tirthankara (Jainism)

"Respect for all life is the foundation." The Great Law of Peace, "All things are our relatives; what we do to everything, we do to ourselves. All is really One." Black Elk, and "Do not wrong or hate your neighbor. For it is not he who you wrong, but yourself." Pima proverb. (Native American Spirituality)

"The law imprinted on the hearts of all men is to love the members of society as themselves." (Roman pagan religion)

"The heart of the person before you is a mirror. See there your own form" Munetada Kurozumi and "Be charitable to all beings, love is the representative of God." Ko-ji-ki Hachiman Kasuga (Shintoism)

"Compassion-mercy and religion are the support of the entire world." Japji Sahib, "Don't create enmity with anyone as God is within everyone." Guru Arjan Devji 259, and "No one is my enemy, none a stranger and everyone is my friend." Guru Arjan Dev : AG 1299 (Sikhism)

"The basis of Sufism is consideration of the hearts and feelings of others. If you haven't the will to gladden someone's heart, then at least beware lest you hurt someone's heart, for on our path, no sin exists but this." Dr. Javad Nurbakhsh, Master of the Nimatullahi Sufi Order. (Sufism, a subset of Islam)

"Regard your neighbor's gain as your gain, and your neighbor's loss as your own loss." Tai Shang Kan Yin P'ien and "To those who are good to me, I am good; to those who are not good to me, I am also good. Thus all get to be good." (Taosim)

"An it harm no one, do what thou wilt" (i.e. do what ever you will, as long as it harms nobody, including yourself). This is called the Wiccan Rede (Wicca)

"One going to take a pointed stick to pinch a baby bird should first try it on himself to feel how it hurts." (Yoruba, Nigeria)

"That nature alone is good which refrains from doing to another whatsoever is not good for itself." Dadisten-I-dinik, 94:5 and "Whatever is disagreeable to yourself do not do unto others." Shayast-na-Shayast 13:29 (Zoroastrianism)

Socrates: "Do not do to others that which would anger you if others did it to you." (Greece; 5th century BCE), Plato: "May I do to others as I would that they should do unto me." (Greece; 4th century BCE), and Seneca, a Roman Stoic philosopher: "Treat your inferiors as you would be treated by your superiors," Epistle to Lucilius 47:11 (Rome; 1st century CE) (Greek and Roman philosophy, the cornerstone of Western Civilization)

That was a long list, but I wanted to include them all; even then, I feel sure with enough research I could find as many more adaptations of the Golden Rule: *12 So in everything, do to others what you would have them do to you, for this sums up the Law and the Prophets.* (Matthew 7:12, NIV) Sum up the law and prophets indeed! It is the foundation of every religion in the world, because every religion ultimately seeks to know and honor the one True God and this is the core message he wants all of humanity to receive and enact in their hearts, minds, and bodies. "Love your neighbor as yourself." (Leviticus 19:18)

Romans 1:20 from The Voice states, *20 From the beginning, creation in its magnificence enlightens us to His nature. Creation itself makes His undying power and divine identity clear, even though they are invisible; and it voids the excuses and ignorant claims of these people 21 because, despite the fact that they knew the one true God, they have failed to show the love, honor, and appreciation due to the One who created them! Instead, their lives are consumed by vain thoughts that poison their foolish hearts.* (Scripture taken from The Voice™. Copyright © 2008 by Ecclesia Bible Society. Used by permission. All rights reserved.) Almost every spiritual tradition, culture, and religion around the world recognizes the Creator, yet some individuals have always chosen rebellion or indifference to Him. This verse also implies that those who did/do acknowledge their Creator and give Him thanks and praise, who live by His law of love, who seek Him are ok, even if they don't pin the right brand on their lapel.

Now let us return to John 14:6. I want to show you a different way to interpret that verse that not only avoids crusades and holy wars, but reveals a whole new vision of the Bible itself. When I taught LSAT classes for potential law school students, one of our subjects was called formal logic. Formal logic is an established pattern of thinking using a series of "if-then" statements to arrive at a true and logical conclusion. Let us apply that to this verse. If one believes that Jesus is God incarnate or the Son of God who is equal to the Father, then this is how it goes:

$$\text{If Jesus} \longrightarrow \text{God}$$

$$\text{If God} \longrightarrow \text{Love}$$

$$\text{If Jesus} \longrightarrow \text{Love}$$

If Jesus equals God and God is love, then Jesus is Love. Therefore, that cornerstone verse could with no change in meaning read, "Love is the way, the truth and the life; no one comes to the Father except through love." I believe when Jesus said this, he was not using the "I" to refer to his human, mortal form, but to the God-essence within him, or simply put, "love." If the "no one" was in fact meant to be absolute, then it would indeed exclude all of those who lived before the time of Jesus, even Noah, Abraham, and Moses. I doubt readers take it to mean that. And various church leaders have come up with a host of theories on how Jesus's statement could be absolute and still have a saving window for the great pillars of faith, but none can be substantiated. What fits with hundreds of other verses, what fits with the character of God, and also that which can be logically derived is this–that Love is the way, the truth and the life. Love is the way to the Father.

Another verse often used to beat people over the head with is found in Romans 6:23. *²³ For the wages of sin is death, but the gift of God is eternal life in Christ Jesus our Lord.* (NIV) Evangelists interpret this verse, "You're going to hell if you don't believe in Jesus," but that is not at all what it states! Note the significant difference in the qualifying term from the first half to the second–*eternal* only appears in the second half of the verse. There is no mention or threat of punishment nor eternal death, only the promise of eternal life. *The wages of sin is death* refers to a physical death. There is sin in the world, therefore at some point or another everyone's body will die. Sometimes the preponderance of sin within an individual's heart, mind, and soul, brings about that death sooner than it would otherwise occur. We know that people who engage in criminal activity, for example, often meet untimely deaths. Likewise, worry, stress, and anxiety take a heavy toll on people's health. We have already discussed how fear of certain manifestations has a tendency to act like a magnet attracting those very outcomes. But whether we bring it on ourselves or we do everything right, because there are entities and motivations other than love at work in the world, we will eventually all die an earthly death. This verse does NOT mention hell, torment, or punishment; it simply says everyone will die one day. It is the second half of the verse we need to focus on - *the gift of God is eternal life!* Jesus Christ, along with prophets from various times and places, came to bring us that good news. If we live in Christ, then we live in love, and vise-versa; it is God's love that saves us, not anything we do ourselves. It is God's will that we embrace love, and in doing so we are accepting that gift of eternal life.

So, what if I am wrong? Most certainly I am wrong about something because no one knows it all. Being proven wrong keeps one humble, and humility is a virtue. The Shroud of Turin is an amazing, mysterious artifact that seems to verify the resurrection of Jesus, but if it were proven to be a forgery, my faith would not be shaken. If it were discovered that Jesus actually had been married to Mary Magdalene as is supposed in "The De Vinci Code," it wouldn't bother me in the least. I do not understand what kind of shallow faith these people have to think such a revelation would rock the Christian world. What difference would it make if Jesus had a wife or even fathered a child? Would it make his miracles any less miraculous? Would it make his teachings any less wonderful and wise? Would it lessen his sacrifice on the cross? Certainly not. What if someone could prove that Mary was in fact not a virgin at the time of Jesus's birth or that he was never resurrected from the dead; what if he had just been a regular man, not God or even the Son of God? Even that would not move me. My faith is not based on the words in a book, the creed or doctrine of a church, or the teachings of any priest or pastor. It is cemented in my relationship with Yahweh, Elohim, Allah, All Glorious, Great Spirit, the Divine Creator of all, Abba. It is as real to me as my relationship with my own parents and children, and I know my God as well as I know my human family.

I realize that not everyone had/has the kind of relationship with their parents that I enjoyed. They were everything God intended parents to be, and I want to take just a moment to explain what that is. It is called unconditional love, and even Jesus assumed that relationship was a given. *"If you, then, though you are evil, know how to give good gifts to your children, how much more will your Father in heaven give good gifts to those who ask him!"* (Matt 7:11, NIV) Unfortunately, some parents ignore, neglect, and abuse their own children, the greatest gift that God can bestow a person on this earth. Jesus had a word for those people too: *"It would be better for them to be thrown into the sea with a millstone tied around their neck than to cause one of these little ones to stumble."* (Luke 17:2, NIV) *Jesus said, "Let the little children come to me, and do not hinder them, for the kingdom of heaven belongs to such as these."* (Matt 19:14, NIV) *"Take heed that ye despise not one of these little ones; for I say unto you, That in heaven their angels do always behold the face of my Father which is in heaven."* (Matt 18:10, NIV) *"Even so it is not the will of your Father which is in heaven, that one of these little ones should perish."* (Matt 18:14, NIV) And repeated in Luke 17:2 *"It were better for him that a millstone were hanged about his neck, and he cast into the sea, than that he should offend one of these little ones."* (NIV)

I not only denote biological mothers and fathers, but step-parents, adoptive parents, foster parents, and society at large that so regularly abuses and discards our most precious resource–our children. There are actually adults who consider themselves to be pious and religious who disown the fruit of their loins. I have heard them say things like, "No child of mine is going to be gay!" "My child isn't going to marry a person of a different race!" "I won't have a child who wants to leave my religion!" "I won't tolerate a kid who does drugs!" "If my daughter gets pregnant, I'll kick her out!" Then their like-minded friends support them, and there is an alarmingly growing number of homeless youth because of it. "It's called tough love; you have to teach them-" NO! It's called pride, fear, intolerance, indifference, and anything but love. Real "tough love" is when you tough it out and love that child unconditionally despite anything he/she does that displeases you. If God were to give you a dose of that kind of "tough love" and abandon you for even one second, the bond that holds the atoms and molecules of your body together would dissolve and you would disintegrate into a pile of dust. Yes, you have to teach them—you have to engrave on their hearts with your every word and action how much God loves them and how much you love them, equipping them with the assurance that your love for them will never fail. Instruct, guide, discipline, certainly! You don't just let them run out into traffic to be hit by a car. Boundaries must be set. But the only thing tossing your child out the door teaches him is that you never really loved him to begin with. "Love never fails." (1 Cor. 13:8, NIV) One who discards his child has failed monumentally!

I am not talking about the parents of a 24 year living at home old who would rather lie on the couch than get a job and contribute to the household—it is time that chick leaves the nest. I mean parents, step-parents, and guardians of teens and younger who are tired of being parents (selfishness), or think it's too hard (fear of inadequacy), or say it's my way or the highway (pride and selfishness). If your child has an addiction, emotional or psychological problem, or is in trouble with the law, you get him or her the help they need; you don't discard them just because they are trying to find their own way and discover their place in the world. That is no kind of love, tough or otherwise.

And we as a society devalue our children. We say that we love them but place no priority on public education, healthcare, or food programs for children. We don't do enough to stop child trafficking or slave labor or child abuse and molestation. We just try to pretend they don't exist. We ignore kids living in poverty and provide them with few alternatives to gangs. Then someone says, "I love *my* children, but *those people's* children are not *my* responsibility. *I* shouldn't have to do anything for *them*." Jesus disagrees with you. Matthew 25:34-46

> [34] "Then the King will say to those on his right, 'Come, you who are blessed by my Father; take your inheritance, the kingdom prepared for you since the creation of the world. [35] For I was hungry and you gave me something to

eat, I was thirsty and you gave me something to drink, I was a stranger and you invited me in, ³⁶ I needed clothes and you clothed me, I was sick and you looked after me, I was in prison and you came to visit me.'

³⁷ "Then the righteous will answer him, 'Lord, when did we see you hungry and feed you, or thirsty and give you something to drink? ³⁸ When did we see you a stranger and invite you in, or needing clothes and clothe you? ³⁹ When did we see you sick or in prison and go to visit you?'

⁴⁰ "The King will reply, 'Truly I tell you, whatever you did for one of the least of these brothers and sisters of mine, you did for me.'

⁴¹ "Then he will say to those on his left, 'Depart from me, you who are cursed, into the eternal fire prepared for the devil and his angels. ⁴² For I was hungry and you gave me nothing to eat, I was thirsty and you gave me nothing to drink, ⁴³ I was a stranger and you did not invite me in, I needed clothes and you did not clothe me, I was sick and in prison and you did not look after me.'

⁴⁴ "They also will answer, 'Lord, when did we see you hungry or thirsty or a stranger or needing clothes or sick or in prison, and did not help you?'

⁴⁵ "He will reply, 'Truly I tell you, whatever you did not do for one of the least of these, you did not do for me.'

⁴⁶ "Then they will go away to eternal punishment, but the righteous to eternal life." (NIV)

This applies to every human on the planet; how much more it applies to our children! Yes, *our* children, the fruit of humanity, our greatest resource, our most cherished blessing, and, yes, "the least of these." When I was a little child we sang a song that is very much needed in our world today: "Jesus loves the little children, all the children of the world. Red and yellow, black and white, they are precious in his sight; Jesus loves the little children of the world." And yet we discard and disregard them—sometimes even the ones born of our flesh.

Unfortunately, there are people today, as there have been throughout time, who simply do not receive the intended image of God as a loving father, because they never had one. And when I speak of my relationship with the Heavenly Father in that way, it may be a stretch for some to comprehend it. Nevertheless, God promotes reconciliation; that is a primary reason Jesus came to earth, to reconcile mankind to our Creator. For children and parents, of any age, whose relationship is or has been dysfunctional, it is not too late to build bridges and began a healing process. If you have that situation in your family, I encourage you to forgive yourself and the family member who hurt or abandoned you. Forgiveness is a powerful, freeing exercise that is a prerequisite to enjoying the abundant life of peace and joy that God intends for you to live.

The Bible, along with other spiritual manuscripts and sacred texts (including those removed by the Counsel of Nicaea), were inspired by God; therefore, they contain truth. But they were also written by men with the inherent potential for error, both in the texts and especially in their translations and interpretations. Throughout 2000 years of history, various generations and nations have adopted and adapted the Bible to fit their culture, modifying their interpretations to meet the norms of their societies. For example, this is how in the 1800s Christians used the Bible both to defend and condemn slavery. I know there are those who believe that God himself wrote every word of the English Bible then dropped it out of Heaven onto King James' desk, ready to go, but that simply is not true. It was written, added to, edited by, translated by, and abbreviated by fallible men (and perhaps a few women) and there may be things that came out wrong or incomplete during that process. But there is one theme that dominates, from cover to cover, author to author, book to book, and of this there can be no doubt: it is God's will and purpose that we live in a spirit of love, not in a spirit of fear.

I believe Jesus is God in human form, that he was inexplicably conceived in Mary's womb, that he performed the recorded miracles and many more, and that he died, was buried, and rose back to life on the third day. But I admit I could be wrong. It is possible that one day it will be discovered or revealed that he was just a man. However that would not shake me, because the message he taught, that the Infinite Power of the Ages loves each and every human soul who ever lived or ever will live on this planet, and that it is His utmost desire that we love one another–that message is enough.

WHO ARE WE?

³ When I consider your heavens,
the work of your fingers,
the moon and the stars,
which you have set in place,
⁴ what is mankind that you are mindful of them,
human beings that you care for them? Psalms 8:3-4, NIV

"What strange beings we are! That sitting in hell at the
bottom of the dark, we're afraid of our own immortality."
Rumi

Perhaps the most important questions we can ever hope to answer include,
"Who are we, where did we come from, and why are we here?" Most people
assume that there are only two diametrically opposed possibilities—creation
and evolution. Even for those who propose that our ancestors traveled
to earth from another planet, people on that world had to have had an
origin as well. I propose to the readers that those two possibilities are not
mutually exclusive at all, that we have grossly misinterpreted both, and that
we were in fact intended by our Creator to be abundantly more than we

have thus far become. The key to understanding the answers to these vital questions lies in forgetting everything you ever learned about creation and everything you ever learned about evolution and to discover anew, without prejudice in either direction. Let us go back to the beginning.

The Jewish Torah and the Christian Bible are not science texts, and despite the narrow-minded persistence of some, they do not claim to be. They were designed to be spiritual guides, written in a time pre-dating modern science, and do not actually attempt to explain geologically or biologically how the earth, stars, plants, and creatures were made. The point of the first chapters of Genesis is to inform the people that they were not accidents, but that they, their world, and the heavenly bodies were purposefully created by the Great I Am. The ancient texts rely on allegories and stories the readers of Moses' time could understand and relate to. We, living in an era of scientific discovery that includes particles of matter our ancestors didn't even know existed, should approach the scriptures from a different perspective.

Take, for instance, Genesis 2:7–*Then the Lord God formed a man from the dust of the ground and breathed into his nostrils the breath of life, and the man became a living being.* Forget the image of big, human-like hands scooping up clay and fashioning a man-like a sculpture, then blowing on the figure to magically transform it into a living being. Let's read this verse in light of modern knowledge. Almost 99% of the human body is made up of these six elements: oxygen (65% by mass), carbon (18%), hydrogen (10%), nitrogen (3%), calcium (1.4%) and phosphorous (1.1%), with about 0.85% composed of potassium, sulfur, sodium, chlorine, and magnesium. The other 0.15% consists of trace elements. Now consider that all of these elements are also present in soil. Essentially, what God did was to use the same chemical elements found in the dust of the ground to create a body for us. Genesis 2:19 tells us that God used those same elements found on the surface of the earth to generate all the other creatures as well. *Now the Lord God had formed out of the ground all the wild animals and all the birds in the sky.* (NIV) This does not mean that the animals mysteriously rose up out of the ground fully formed. Think about the knowledge God imparted to Moses, author of the book of Genesis–that the elements of the earth, unseen to mankind at that time, were the very building blocks He used to fashion the creatures of the air, land, and sea, and the same chemicals He used to form humans. But beyond Moses' time, God was speaking to our time, a time where these chemical elements would be known and studied. It was as if the Divine Spirit inspired Moses to write these words so that people of today would see and understand in light of our discoveries.

One controversy surrounds the fundamentalists' view that the entire creation of the universe occurred in six, twenty-four-hour days, as a strict, literal reading of Genesis chapter one would suggest. This proposal also attempts to date the earth based on lineages listed and supposed live-spans of those lineages, therefore leading this school of theology to arrive at a planetary age of approximately 6,000 years. (The Great Sphinx is estimated to be more than 10,000 years old.) These believers are frequently scoffed at by intellectuals causing them to further attack science, denying even the most obvious facts. The problem lies in an improper approach to and interpretation of the scriptures. Psalms 90:4 explains, *A thousand years in your sight are like a day that has just gone by, or like a watch in the night.* (NIV) The Infinite God does not view time in the same way we do. Many more enlightened followers of the Judea-Muslim-Christian texts have embraced what they call the Long-Day Theory of Creation. The "days" described in Genesis refer to eons or epochs, long periods of time as we count it. Additionally, using the lineages from Adam to Jesus to try to calculate the age of the earth is more than problematic. The "begats", as they are often referred to, likely only include those decedents deemed important enough to mention. In the old Jewish tradition, "son of" or "father of" could denote people who were generations apart. Recall that Jesus was often called "son of David," and faithful Hebrews of his time called themselves "sons of Abraham." This is not a reliable or even a reasonable method to determine the age of the planet or even how long man has been around.

We would do well to recognize established scientific facts. The earth is millions of years old and modern humans have inhabited it for approximately 200,000 years. These are reliably provable facts, but they do not in any real way contradict the belief that a Supreme Being is responsible for the existence of the universe and ourselves.

Charles Darwin's theory of evolution by natural selection, first revealed in his book "On the Origin of Species" in 1859, is the process by which organisms change over time as a result of mutations in heritable physical or behavioral traits. Changes that allow an organism to better adapt to its environment will help it survive and have more offspring, while those that do not will be discarded by nature. (Note: if you have accepted my premise that God created everything that is, inhabits all things, and everything in the universe resides within His infinite being, then to say "nature" selects or does anything, is to say that God selects or determines that outcome. God and nature are one.) The theory has some substantiated evidence in the fossil record as well as similarities in DNA between like species. Examples include the evolution of the horse and whale. Anyone can conclude that the similarities between wooly mammoths and modern elephants suggest the species changed and adapted to a warming climate. The smaller, less hairy varieties thrived in the new environment while those who maintained thick coats of fur and required substantially more vegetation to support their bulk died off or were hunted to the brink by a growing population of humans.

However, when one attempts to apply evolution to all living things on the planet, problems arise. Then the validity of the theory becomes little more than conjecture with a few fossils to point to and a lot of faith on the part of the evolution believer. After a hundred and fifty years of searching, no hard evidence has been uncovered, no multitude of fossilized "missing links" found, only a stubborn set of scientists and textbook authors who wish to conclude the theory is a fact simply because they don't have a better one. But the fantastical leap occurs with the supposition that all life began in a blob of genetic goo that was somehow randomly sparked into living material by an accidental contact with electricity in the atmosphere. Many prominent scientists disagreed with Darwin then and still do today.

"Darwin's theory is not inductive—not based on a series of acknowledged facts pointing to a general conclusion." said Adam Sedgwick (1785–1873), of Cambridge University, a British geologist and one of the founders of modern geology. Instead it is a conclusion in search of supporting facts. H. S. Lipson (1910–1991), a British physicist who taught at the University of Manchester Institute of Science and Technology observed, *"Evolution became in a sense a scientific religion; almost all scientists have accepted it and many are prepared to 'bend' their observations to fit with it."* Cambridge University zoologist Leonard Harrison Matthews (1901–1986) considered it this way: *"Evolution is the backbone of biology and biology is thus in the*

peculiar position of being a science founded on unproven theory—is it then a science or a faith? Belief in the theory of evolution is thus exactly parallel to belief in special creation—both are concepts which believers know to be true, but neither, up to the present, has been capable of proof.” Sir Fred Hoyle (1915–2001), a British astronomer from Cambridge University who formed the theory of stellar nucleosynthesis declared, *“The chance that higher life forms might have emerged in this way is comparable with the chance that a tornado sweeping through a junkyard might assemble a Boeing 747 from the materials therein. I am at a loss to understand biologists’ widespread compulsion to deny what seems to me to be obvious.”* Neither is Michael Denton (1943–), British biochemist, senior fellow at the Center for Science and Culture, convinced of the theory’s validity: *“Ultimately the Darwinian theory of evolution is no more or less than the great cosmogenic myth of the twentieth century. The truth is that despite the prestige of evolutionary theory and the tremendous intellectual effort directed towards reducing living systems to the confines of Darwinian thought, nature refuses to be imprisoned. In the final analysis we still know very little about how new forms of life arise.”*

Francis Crick, the Nobel Prize-winning co-discoverer of the DNA double helix, believed that the eloquence of life’s building blocks has to be the result of something more than arbitrary mutations and a fortuitous fluke of nature. Late in life, Crick risking his reputation as a scientist, stated publicly, “An *honest* man, armed with all the knowledge available to us now, could only state that in some sense, the origin of life appears at the moment to be almost a miracle.” When you look at the complexity of life on earth and the intricacies of even one part of the body–the eye–that allow us and other creatures to see and process the information taken in by that organ, the prospect that it all started by some chance occurrence followed by billions of chance occurrences that by today allow an eagle from half a mile up in the sky to spot a rabbit two miles away, that allow a human to perceive a ball hurling toward him with enough precision to swing a bat and strike it dead center propelling it over a fence ninety yards away, is fantastical. Mathematical odds strongly favor creation by design over the shot in the dark supposition.

Does this mean we throw out everything Darwin hypothesized? Not necessarily. He could very well have been right on many points, but the largest problem facing society today is how evolutionists twisted his writings and their intended purposes into the prevailing Social Darwinism culture from which we must now break free. The theory sometimes described as "survival of the fittest," can be misleading according Briana Pobiner, an anthropologist and educator at the Smithsonian Institution National Museum of Natural History in Washington, D.C. "Fitness" refers not to an organism's strength or athletic ability, but rather the ability to survive and reproduce. Social Darwinism has applied the concept that only the roughest, toughest, individuals, those who excel in competition, those who are strong enough to beat back all comers, are the ones who survive and ultimately "win." This idea has pressed its way into the business world, the economy, politics, and even family dynamics. This was NOT what Darwin taught, nor was it his intention that human societies move away from cooperation toward conflict and intense competition. That conflated infiltration into human society has been highly detrimental and the best modern science of today tells us it has no foundation in fact.

Natural scientists of the twenty-first century have discovered and documented scores of examples of how nature actually operates in cooperation much more than in competition. Creatures ranging from amoebas to elephants live in complex societies. Ant colonies display a highly organized civilization in which each member works for the benefit of the group. Ravens guide wolves to prey, pilot fish clean sharks' teeth, Columbian tarantulas and small dotted humming frogs share dens to the benefit of both (despite the fact that the larger tarantula could easily eat the frog); herbivores specialize in upper leaves, lower leaves, tall grasses, short grasses, etc. so that each has a niche and they are not all fighting over the same food source. Even predator animals benefit prey animals by thinning herds of the weak and sick allowing the genetically stronger members to reproduce. The list goes on. This is true in the plant world as well. Peter Wohlleben, a German forester, has written a 2016 book, *The Hidden Life of Trees: What They Feel, How They Communicate—Discoveries from a Secret World*, that presents extraordinary evidence of cooperation between trees in a forest, including phenomena ranging from how the root systems of a whole forest interconnect to electrical and chemical signals released from a tree being attacked by insects to warn the other trees. Certainly competition exists in nature, but we are now discovering that it is cooperation that is the more pervasive force and the one that keeps the world in balance.

Survival of the fittest was never intended to be applied to human society, and it has been a disastrous experiment. Such a notion that one must be ruthless to survive is in total contradiction to the purpose for which we were created. Our design was as a being possessing a tremendous capacity for compassion. Jesus listed the qualities the Divine Father deems highest, noblest, and to be strived for in his Beatitudes (Matthew 5:3-10):

> [3] "Blessed are the poor in spirit,
>   for theirs is the kingdom of heaven.
> [4] Blessed are those who mourn,
>   for they will be comforted.
> [5] Blessed are the meek,
>   for they will inherit the earth.
> [6] Blessed are those who hunger and thirst for righteousness,
>   for they will be filled.
> [7] Blessed are the merciful,
>   for they will be shown mercy.
> [8] Blessed are the pure in heart,
>   for they will see God.
> [9] Blessed are the peacemakers,
>   for they will be called children of God.
> [10] Blessed are those who are persecuted because of righteousness,
>   for theirs is the kingdom of heaven. (NIV)

Today some of the most successful companies are moving away from the failed theory of conflict and competition and adopting practices that promote cooperation and teamwork. We are seeing that applying Darwin's theories to human society was a wretched mistake that brought out our darkest tendencies while suppressing our better angels. Nineteenth century British author Charles Dickens was one of the first to make this case in his novels of social justice. *"I looked at the stars, and considered how awful it would be for a man to turn his face up to them as he froze to death, and see no help or pity in all the glittering multitude."*

There is no scientifically proven chain of evolutionary events tracing from "goo to you", despite a hundred and fifty years of searching for them, but there are examples we have observed of species mutation. It happens very commonly in viruses and bacteria, which is why researchers are constantly having to develop new flu vaccines for the new influenza strains. It has been noted in insects that develop a resistance to certain chemicals used to control their populations. Homeowners find that they need to switch brands to kill the new "super roaches" that no longer respond to the old spray. It has happened in humans as some people now never develop wisdom teeth or are born without an appendix.

Then there is the famous example of the peppered moths in London. Before 1811 these moths were all light colored with some dark spots. But at that time air pollution from coal was turning all of the city's buildings black, and white moths resting on the bricks were easily picked off by birds. By 1848 it was noted that many these moths were then of the black variety. In 1895 the peppered moth population stood at 98% black variety with only 2% white. From 1953 to 1956 Bernard Kettlewell investigated the moth adaptation concluding that moths in clean environments such as the country side appeared much more in the light colored version while those in polluted places such as Birmingham, England, were almost exclusively black. These findings were hailed as evidence for evolution, but were they really?

Kettlewell's experiments with the two varieties of moth and two varieties of birds that fed on them were reproduced in 1965 and 1969 by Theodore David Sargent, however this time with different results, showing no difference in the color of moth against a light or dark tree and which bird ate it. Others in the scientific community looked on Kettlewell with skepticism as well. And even though the moths did change colors over the course of the 1800s, there were no DNA studies performed as DNA had not been discovered yet. A change in pigmentation does not equal a fundamental alteration of the species, therefore while it can be a case for adaptation, it does not constitute evidence for evolution. We know, for example, that brown eye color is a dominate trait. In a population of blue-eyed people, parents both possessing the recessive gene with pass it on to their children, but when you start introducing brown eye color into the mix, it will eventually become dominate in the line of decedents. Could the moths' coloring be as simple as a change in which gene was dominant?

Now let us consider these verses from Genesis Chapter One.

> [11] Then God said, "Let the land produce vegetation: seed-bearing plants and trees on the land that bear fruit with seed in it, according to their various kinds."

> [20] And God said, "Let the water teem with living creatures, and let birds fly above the earth across the vault of the sky." [21] So God created the great creatures of the sea and every living thing with which the water teems and that moves about in it, according to their kinds, and every winged bird according to its kind."

> [24] And God said, "Let the land produce living creatures according to their kinds: the livestock, the creatures that move along the ground, and the wild animals, each according to its kind." (NIV)

Here we must ask what is meant by their "kind"? Biology divides living things into both broad and narrow categories: Domain (Archea, Eubacteria, Eukaryote), Kingdom (Plantae, Animalia, Fungi, Protists, Eubacteria, Archaebacteria), Phylum, Class, Order, Family, Genus, and Species–the smallest classification. So, when God said "kind" it matters which category He meant. We know that not every plant and animal appeared on earth at the same time, but rather with millions of years in between. Some were successful, such as jellyfish, one of the earliest complex life forms that is still around in large numbers today. Others became extinct and were replaced, usually, by a more sophisticated life form. Insects have survived for eons with only small changes while amphibians, reptiles, birds, marsupials, and mammals have gone through tremendous alterations, extinction and emergence events. So, when God said according to their "kind", perhaps that meant "family". Was it Phylum? For animals those are invertebrates, fish, birds, reptiles, amphibians, and mammals. Maybe class–for mammals those are monotremes, marsupials, and the largest group, placental mammals. Perhaps He meant Order–there are 19 orders of mammals–Ungulata (hoofed animals), Carnivora (including canines, cats, bears, and others), Cetacea (whales and porpoises), Chiroptera (bats), Dermoptera (flying lemurs), Edentata (toothless mammals such as sloths and anteaters), Hyracoidae (whose only living family is hyraxes), Lagomorpha (pikas, hares, and rabbits), Marsupialia (pouched animals), Monotremata (egg-laying mammals), Perissodactyla (odd-toed hoofed animals such as equines and tapirs), Pholidata (pangolins are the only family), Pinnipedia (seals and walruses), Primates, Proboscidea (elephants), Rodentia (gnawing mammals), Sirenia (dugongs and manatees), and Tubulidentata (aardvarks).

I will not start the breakdown into Family, Genus, and Species. But it is worth considering that when God said "according to their kind" He was not referring to Species, but something up the classification line. This could then allow for mutations, changes, alterations, adaptations that developed within that order of animal. Say, for example, God created Eohippus, the first horse. Then over the course of millions of years the creature adapted to changing climate, habitat, food and predator situations. It not only evolved but branched out into donkeys, zebras, ponies, and horses. Depending on where on the planet the populations migrated to, the slow genetic changes help suit that variety of equine to its environment. There is a good deal of fossil evidence to support a line of equines from Eohippus to the modern horse, but no evidence to support some long extinct non-equine ancestor evolving into Eohippus. Therefore, the phrase "according to their kind" is significant in allowing for some measure of evolution without the erroneous conclusion that all life is happenstance.

Then the question returns to how the genetic alterations occurred. Were they pure random, simply luck of the draw? Most observed mutations, such as a cow born with two heads, do nothing to advance the species. They typically are not traits passed on to off-spring, if there even are off-spring. How would a non-sentient insect such as a moth know it needed to change colors to avoid being eaten? How would the wooly rhino determine it needed to phase out that heavy coat when the ice sheets receded and the climate warmed? If you answer, "Nature selected them," then you are representing nature as an intelligent force. The sheer insistence on the arbitrary acceptance of these genetic shifts is what makes no logical sense.

But when you consider that those mutations and adaptations were by design, that a benevolent, all-powerful intelligence was what triggered the adjustments, that it was God modifying His creation, culling life-forms to make way for newer ones, adapting a specific Order or Genus or Species to be better suited for an earth in flux, then we see the genius in nature, not an arbitrary accident. When we put aside the myth that mankind is no more that the result of a succession of unplanned, purposeless flukes of genetics, then we can start to look at the truth of who we are and why we are here.

The most controversial aspect of Darwin's theory is the decent of man– did we really evolve from apes? New scientists are looking to DNA for the answers and their discoveries have been quite surprising. In 1987, in the Caucus region of Russia, archeologists discovered the completely preserved body of a Neanderthal infant girl who lived about 30,000 years ago during the last ice age. Using forensic techniques researchers extracted and tested her mitochondrial DNA. This form of DNA is significant because it is passed directly from mother to off-spring with none of the individual trait-forming variations. This means that the mitochondrial DNA lines in our bodies today are the direct descendants, and exact matches, of the mitochondrial DNA of the first woman. (Genetic science has determined as fact that our entire species has descended from one woman, aptly named Eve.) Russian and Swedish scientists tested the Neanderthal infant's DNA to see how similar hers was to that of modern-day humans, and to determine if modern man could have evolved from Neanderthals.

In 2000 researchers at the University of Glasgow Human Identification Centre published the results of their investigation in the peer-reviewed journal *Nature*. The meaning derived from this conclusion was unmistakable and their report directly stated that modern humans "were not, in fact, descended from Neanderthals." That is now made clear from mitochondrial DNA test results but also from the fossil record that indicated Neanderthals lived at a time period overlapping that of Anatomically Modern Humans (AMHs). Therefore the notion that Neanderthals were a link in the chain of human evolution has been thoroughly disproven.

Scientists now generally agree that Anatomically Modern Humans, who were once called Cro-Magnon Man, are the same genetically as

Homo sapiens, the designation given to modern humans. Our fully human ancestors appeared on this earth approximately 200,000 years ago with all the same functions and systems, with advanced speech capabilities and large frontal lobe brains, equipped with extraordinary abilities such as intuition, compassion, empathy, love and self-healing–everything we have today. Additionally, the fact that members of our species, *Homo sapiens*, haven't changed since our earliest ancestors first appeared in the fossil record poses a problem for the traditional story of evolution, which is based upon slow changes over long periods of time. Other species have risen and fallen within this 200,000 year period and yet man has remained genetically unaltered.

Modern genetic studies do reveal that while we did not descend from Neanderthals, about 4% of people living today, especially of European and Middle Eastern origin, do have some Neanderthal DNA. This is the result of interbreeding that occurred on a small scale during the period that both species shared the earth. One question those who maintain a literal interpretation of Genesis have difficulty answering is that of Cain's wife. In the story after Cain killed his brother Abel, he was banished from his home and was afraid that whoever found him would kill him, so God put a mark on him to ensure his safety. Then he traveled to the land of Nod, east of Eden, and lived with the people there, taking a wife and fathering children. So if Adam and Eve were the first *Homo sapiens*, fully modern humans, who were these "people" Cain lived with and married into? Even the strictest fundamentalists allow that Adam and Eve had more children than just the three sons mentioned in Genesis–there would by necessity had to have been some daughters. And incest at that point would not have been a genetic problem since Eve contained in her DNA all the genetic possibilities unlike people today whose genetic prospects have been greatly narrowed. But it is not feasible that Eve had enough children to populate more than one community. Therefore, the obvious answer to the question is that Cain's wife was a Neanderthal woman. Although they did not have the capacity for complex speech, they could communicate, use tools, and lived in organized societies.

We share 98% of our DNA with chimpanzees, and it is that other 2% that makes us uniquely human. Plotting the Human genome provided revolutionary information about us. These genetic scientists discovered several key changes that occurred all at once. In human chromosome two there suddenly appeared genes responsible for the neocortex, the part of the brain that makes us uniquely human, the center for empathy, sympathy and compassion, and complex language. No other form of life has these specific genes. Another of the modifications that makes us human is found in chromosome seven, giving us the ability for complex speech. Two DNA letters were switched at exactly the same time giving us the ability to connect our tongue and mouth with speech centers in our brain and it hasn't changed since. In the seventy-five million year history of the chimpanzee, this mutation never occurred, not once, but when it came time for humans, there it was simultaneously with chromosome two's enhancement of the neocortex. Scientists further explain that the way the genes were modified, with a slight tweaking of the code to remove any redundant features and make it strong and stable, demonstrates intentionality. Theses dramatic changes in DNA did not appear gradually, slowly over time, but all at the same time. These discoveries are peer reviewed science but they have not made it into our textbooks or mainstream documentaries yet because they are so new and there is a resistance by some in the scientific community to publicize anything that doesn't support Darwin.[3]

Darwin's theory of evolution made us feel small, insignificant, and purposeless. It chipped away at the preciousness and immense value of life. It so permeated twentieth century thought that even those who most adamantly opposed Darwin, the religious fundamentalists, (perhaps subconsciously) used his principles to support their own racial prejudices, believing their race to be genetically superior to others, even so far as Nazism teaching that Jews were a subhuman species, therefore it was ok to kill them. If everything is random, if there is no rhyme or reason, if it is a kill or be killed world, then what is the point? The question people began to ask in any situation was, "What's in it for *me*? How do *I* benefit from this?" But when we understand that there is a design and a purpose, that every life is precious and valuable, that love, compassion, intuition, and cooperation both with nature and each other are the correct paths for humanity, then the questions become, "What can I *give*? How can I *contribute*?" and these are the right questions.

---

[3] For further reading on these new DNA discoveries, check out *Human by Design* by Gregg Braden.

Accurate science seeks to find the truth; honest religion or spirituality also seeks to find the truth. It is when we stop seeking, thinking we have already discovered all the answers, that we get into trouble. Remember Jesus told us to "keep seeking," and he also declared, *"32 Then you will know the truth, and the truth will set you free."* (John 8:32, NIV) Only by seeking can we find. If our goal is only to perpetuate what we already think, to repudiate facts and argue traditions, then we are no longer seeking truth. We cannot start with the desired conclusion and work backwards; we must examine the evidence and then draw the conclusion.

So now we know what we are *not*: we are not the result of arbitrary occurrences; there is no evidence to support an evolutionary family tree for humans, we did not descend from Neanderthals, the precision and timing that produced the DNA that gives us our uniqueness is not commonplace in nature, and aside from being taller, heavier versions, we have not fundamentally changed in 200,000 years. So what *are* we?

God decided to create this universe because He is creative by nature. Was there a universe before this one? Who knows? There are far more questions than I can ever hope to answer. In the course of that work He fashioned thousands upon thousands of single-cell organisms, plants, and animals as well as geologic features, stars, planets, and heavenly bodies. While some of the simple varieties remained, some did not and more complex ones emerged. Genesis quotes God as saying each and every one was good. But the project was not complete without fulfilling the goal of placing a spiritual being into a physical body, one who could appreciate the creation, and one who could communicate with the Creator.

Genesis 1:27 tells us: *So God created mankind in his own image, in the image of God he created them; male and female he created them.* (NIV) As I mentioned back in part one, this has absolutely nothing to do with physical appearance and everything to do with who we are on the inside. God is creative and He made us creative as well. It is in our very nature to invent, compose, produce, design, engineer, write, dance, paint, etc. We are inspired, artistic, resourceful, knit together with ingenuity and imagination because that is how He planned us to be. The Most High also endued us with the capacity for compassion, empathy, kindness, love, intuition, and much more and He intended us to use them for the betterment of our world and our own selves. He infused us with curiosity so that we would explore His creation and seek Him in nature, mathematics, and science as well as in houses of worship. The Omnipotent Father bestowed upon us some of His very own characteristics, including that of free will. We can decide what we believe, how we feel, what we will think, say, or do in any given situation. The challenge becomes to choose wisely.

Are we the only creatures possessing these qualities? Perhaps not, but we do enjoy them to a greater degree. When we consider higher level animals, we attribute the ability to sing to birds and whales as well as humans. Other primates have been observed problem solving, even using simple tools to accomplish their goal. Wildlife experts have witnessed elephants demonstrating compassion toward other animals, even outside their species, as they attempt to rescue them from harm. Dogs are extremely loyal to their people and stories of how they have saved the lives of children and adults alike abound. Recently in the news was the saga of a young Orca mother whose calf died and she pushed it around for many days keeping its blow-hole out of the water hoping to revive it before in exhaustion she finally gave up. There exists much evidence for expressions of love, devotion, and caring as well as ingenuity within members of the animal kingdom, and yet none of them have composed a symphony or sculpted a *David.* Their technology is very limited whereas ours knows no bounds. *The Lord said, "If as one people speaking the same language they have begun to do this, then nothing they plan to do will be impossible for them.* (Genesis 11:6, NIV)

Do other animals have souls? If by "soul" you mean personality, emotions, and even dreams, the answer is yes. I have been around animals my whole life and can attest to the fact that even beyond the obvious dogs and cats (which any pet owner can confirm), farm animals such as pigs, goats, horses, and cows have their own distinct personalities with preferences for certain company, foods, activities, and display unique mannerisms. They form attachments and bonds which could be described as love, both with each other and the people in their lives. So yes, using that definition of soul, a host of higher functioning birds and animals were clearly endowed with a soul.

It can also be argued that all creatures have a spirit as the term "spirit" is often defined as "God's breath" or "life force" within all things. The

Hebrew word *ru'ach* and the Greek word *pneu'ma* are both translated as "spirit." The Scriptures themselves specify the meaning of those words. For example, Psalm 104:29 states: *"When you [Jehovah] take away their breath [ru'ach], they die and return to the dust."* (NIV) And James 2:26 notes that *"the body without spirit [pneu'ma] is dead."* (NIV) In these verses, "spirit" refers to that which bestows life to a body. Without the spirit, the body is dead. The Bible not only uses the word *ru'ach* to mean "spirit" but also as "force," or life-force. For example, concerning the Flood in Noah's day, God said: *17 I am going to bring floodwaters on the earth to destroy all life under the heavens, every creature that has the breath [ru'ach] of life in it."* (Genesis 6:17, NIV) "Spirit" therefore denotes an invisible force (the spark of life) that animates all living creatures.

What may be different where humans are concerned (and we do not have definitive evidence in this matter), is the eternal nature of our spirit. Aside from beliefs and writings in ancient texts, we have many personal testimonies supporting "life after death." Do animals, too, transcend this life into another plain of existence when the physical body dies? Because of our limited ability to communicate with them, we simply do not know. There does exist a great deal of evidence in manuscripts and near-death experiences to support the continuation of spirit life in human beings. The divine spark in each of us is eternal and will live on in another dimension.

What about the idea of reincarnation, the rebirth of the spirit into a new body? There are those who balk, insisting that belief is inconsistent with the Judeo-Muslim-Christian principle that those who die in good standing with the Almighty go to Heaven when they die while evil people go to hell. Though not being drawn off into the tangent of hell possibilities, I do ask the question, "What makes these two beliefs incompatible?" A fair number of individuals seem to have memories of past lives and that doesn't make them crazy. God is very clear in scriptures that He is the judge; God and God alone decides what path He will send a spirit on when he/she departs their mortal coils. Therefore, it is conceivable – even practical – that babies and young children who did not have the opportunity to live full lives are reborn into new bodies. It is possible that those who lived longer, but were unable to fulfill their purpose, get a second chance. It is even imaginable that people who never had an opportunity to know God could be reborn, and still not conflict with the notion that those who sought the Lord, believed in His goodness, and tried to live in love and compassion in the world are translated into the spiritual realm of Heaven when their spirits leave their bodies behind. As William Shakespeare so aptly wrote it in his play *Hamlet: "There are more things in heaven and earth than are dreamt of in your philosophy."*

So, we are spiritual beings who have a soul and reside in a body, formed to be similar to God in our creativity and potential to love and be loved, destined to live forever in a spiritual kingdom. But we were also all created as unique individuals. Yahweh loves variety as evidenced by creation itself. No two vein patterns in leaves, spot patterns on leopards, stripe arrangements on zebras, pedal arrays on flowers, nor crystalline formations in snowflakes are the same; each is unique. There is more variety in nature than we can contemplate in a library of volumes, but I will choose just one example–the butterfly. Not only are every individual butterfly's wing patterns distinctive, but there are over 20,000 different species of butterfly and at least 160,000 species of moths (not all species have even been identified yet.) Compare that to only around 350 species of primates. Butterflies come in a vast array of colors, designs, sizes, and shapes and every single one–though they live but for a week to a few months–is meticulously fashioned as a one-of-a-kind work of art. Why? In order to fulfill their role in nature, aiding in plant pollination and providing food for other creatures, only a handful of species, one for each ecosystem, is required. So, why so many? Who cares if they all look alike or not? Our Creator cares. He fashioned a dazzling world bursting with breathtaking splendor. He wanted nature to be beautiful for us to appreciate, admire, and find joy in. Every tree, flower, creature that flies, walks, swims, or crawls, and every person is a singular conception sprung from the mind of God.

Therefore, doesn't it make sense that each human would be as different as our fingerprints? Some are tall, others short, plump, thin, athletic, intellectual, extroverted, introverted, gay, straight, bi, trans; hair of black, brown, red, blonde, straight, curly; eyes of ebony, chestnut, blue, green, hazel; different shaped faces, noses, and lips, with diverse skin tones and vocal timbres. We all possess separate styles, likes and dislikes, talents and abilities, interests, opinions, and viewpoints. This is God's design; so why is it that some people, often the staunchly religious, think everyone should be alike? They want to shove people into their mold so they all come out with the "right" hair style, clothing selections, behaviors, choices, and beliefs. They think the whole world should march to the beat of their drum when in reality the Supreme Power intended just the opposite! It doesn't matter if one person wants to wear a hijab and another a sombrero; one a floor-length skirt and another shorts or jeans; one chooses piercings, another tattoos, dyed hair colors, and so on. Some like action books or films while others prefer drama or romance; one lives in the city and the other the country. We are SUPPOSED to be diverse and individual, not cut out of some religious guru's cookie cutter mold; why aren't God's molds, used only once each, good enough? And yet a man of one race supposes himself superior to another, a woman with one belief looks down on those who differ; men deem themselves better than women, the rich above the poor, and the list goes on.

But in God's eyes, every human being in the world is beautiful beyond measure! *I am fearfully and wonderfully made* (Psalm 139:14, NIV). *Your eyes saw my unformed body; all the days ordained for me were written in your book before one of them came to be. [17] How precious to me are your thoughts,[a] God! How vast is the sum of them!* (Psalm 139:16-17, NIV). *For we are the product of His hand, heaven's poetry etched on lives, created in the Anointed, Jesus, to accomplish the good works God arranged long ago* (Ephesians 2:10, Scripture taken from The Voice™. Copyright © 2008 by Ecclesia Bible Society. Used by permission. All rights reserved.) *God saw all that he had made, and it was very good.* (Genesis 1:31NIV)

As an over-the-road truck driver, I have traveled through all 48 contiguous states and have also been privileged to visit Canada, Mexico, and the Bahamas and to this I can attest–they are all beautiful, each in its own special way. I have been surrounded by the reds, oranges, and yellows of the leaves changing in New England, delighted in the sunbeams and salty breezes of white-sand beaches, and winded through majestic snow-capped peaks. I have stood in silent awe on the floor of the Redwood Forest as its bows rose hundreds of feet above, stood in reverent wonder on the rim of the surreal artistry of the Grand Canyon, and been enveloped by a sunrise in the desert southwest casting mesas and plateaus in splendid hues. I have felt the vitality and comfort of familiar forests in the South and East, passed mile after mile of golden fields of grain and pastures of grazing cattle in the Midwest, and meandered through the foggy green round-tops of the ancient Appalachians. My boots have crunched through new snow in picturesque settings and my toes have wiggled in the soft silt of creek beds; I have felt the heat fade into evening cool in the desert and beheld a panorama of countless stars in Big Sky country. From coast to coast, everything my eyes have beheld was beautiful, save the scars and pollution left by man. What mind could have conceived such varied splendor, what power bring it into being? Only Abba, Yahweh, the All in All, the great I Am!

Our Creator did not stop there, but filled this lovely earth with living creatures, each one unique, each its own rare masterpiece. Likewise, every human is beautiful in our individuality, and each equally loved and adored by the Father of Light.

I had parked at a truck stop on a beautiful spring afternoon at a time when I was piecing these revelations together, trying earnestly to comprehend a barrage of facts, feelings, discoveries, and ideas and was still unable to express them in any coherent way. While walking the dog I gazed at nature's beauty with the wonder of a child, considering how God is in everything, when my attention was drawn to a purple wildflower. Taking a moment, I sat on the ground beside it, cradling the delicate blossom in gentle hands. There were thousands like it in view, yet not a one its duplicate. I inhaled its fragrance then brushed its velvety pedals across my face and touched them to my lips thinking, "God is in this flower; He is in the air I breathe, the sunshine on my skin, the breeze that caresses me, even the ground I sit upon." After letting that thought sink in, another rose up from within; "Our God is so awesome that even what we deem mere weeds He crowns with splendor!" God is beauty—He formed all within Himself, painting all with loveliness, reflecting all that He is in the creation. He does this every day because that is who He is: the artist, the canvas, and the painting. If He so marvelously clothes the grass of the field in brilliance, how much more you and I? We are His workmanship; therefore, everyone is beautiful.

"The Lord does not look at the things people look at. People look at the outward appearance, but the Lord looks at the heart." 1 Samuel 16:7 (NIV)

And now it is time to get to the heart of the matter, and in doing so explore how we are beginning to rediscover the way to be more than we are. The ancients placed great significance on one human organ in particular–the heart. Most early civilizations, in both eastern and western culture, viewed the heart as the seat of emotions. Egyptians believed that the heart, rather than the brain, was the source of human wisdom, as well as emotions, memory, the soul and the personality itself. Greek philosopher Aristotle believed that the heart was the source of all vitality, that the heart, rather than the brain, controlled the body, and concluded it was the first organ to come to life and the last to die. Nearly five hundred years later, Galen observed that no other internal organ performed such continuous, hard work as the heart and argued that its expansion and contraction demonstrated its role as an intelligent organ.

In eastern philosophies, Buddhism and Hinduism viewed the heart as the center of life, action, emotion, consciousness, and the soul. It is defined by the principles of transformation that enable us to bridge our earthly and higher aspirations. As the fourth chakra (out of seven) located in the middle of our chest, the heart links the lower and upper chakras (where the physical and spiritual meet), integrating the energies of heaven and earth into one harmonious, coherent whole. According to this belief, when the heart chakra is open, we feel deeply connected to the world around us, filled with love and compassion, accepting of change, and transcending our perceived limitations. If the heart chakra is blocked or closed-off, we are likely to experience difficulty relating to others, giving way to feelings of anger, jealousy, fear or betrayal. Similarly, Chinese medicine views the heart as the supreme ruler responsible for maintaining internal peace and harmony over the entire body.

The Bible is filled with references to the heart as more than a blood pumping muscle, references that today most people view as figurative. Remember how I told you that one of the biggest mistakes we make is to interpret what God meant to be taken figuratively as literal and what He meant to be literal as a figure of speech? Scriptures from Old and New

Testaments spell out many truths about the heart that are shared by all the ancient traditions and that are at last being proven by twenty-first century science!

According to scriptures we believe/trust with our hearts (Psalm 28:7, Romans 10:9, 10), pray in our hearts (Genesis 24:45, 1 Samuel 1:13), think in our hearts (Genesis 6:5, Matthew 15:19), moved to give in our hearts (Exodus 35:21), feel hatred and lust in our hearts (Leviticus 19:17, Numbers 15:39), experience fear in our hearts (Deuteronomy 1:28, Joshua 2:11), love with our hearts (Deuteronomy 6:5, Matthew 22:37), know in our hearts (Deuteronomy 8:5, Joshua 23:14, 1 Kings 2:44), serve God with our hearts (Deuteronomy 11:13, Joshua 22:5, 1 Samuel 12:20), despair in our hearts (Deuteronomy 28:65, Nehemiah 2:2, Romans 9:2), harden our hearts (Joshua 11:20, 1 Samuel 6:6, Mark 6:52), melt our hearts (Psalms 22:14), search our hearts (Judges 5:15,16, Psalms 4:4, Psalms 119:58), discern in our hearts (1 Kings 3:12), change our hearts (1 Kings 8:47, 2 Chronicles 6:37), feel gladness and joy in our hearts (1 Kings 8:66, Psalms 4:7, Acts 2:26), store integrity in our hearts (1 Kings 9:4, Psalms 78:72), desire in our hearts (1 Kings 11:37, Job 17:11, Psalms 20:4), devote our hearts (1 Chronicles 22:19, 2 Chronicles 17:6, Job 11:13), seek with our hearts (2 Chronicles 15:12), work with our hearts (Nehemiah 4:6, Colossians 3:23), sin in our hearts (Job 1:5), give thanks with our heart (Psalms 9:1, Colossians 3:16) speak from our hearts (Psalms 15:2, Matthew 15:18), be instructed by our hearts (Psalms 16:7), meditate in our hearts (Psalms 19:14, Psalms 49:3), sing with our hearts (Psalms 30:12, Ephesians 5:19), doubt in our hearts (Mark 11:23), and many, many other examples. Adjectives are assigned to our hearts throughout the Bible such as weak, strong, hard, soft, deceitful, wicked, prideful, humble, pure, honest, heavy, light, sorrowful, joyful, faithful, true, and so on.

Scriptures describe the heart much the same way that the ancient Egyptians, Greeks, Hindus, Buddhists, and Chinese do—as the most important entity within our bodies, as well as the seat of feelings, emotions, thoughts, and our souls. Then in the seventeenth century medical science determined that the heart was nothing more than a muscle that pumps blood through the body. Suddenly this preponderance of human philosophy, spiritual belief, texts and scriptures were rendered superstitious non-sense and all references to the heart otherwise were relegated to poetic or figurative language not to be taken factually, to the detriment of humanity—until now!

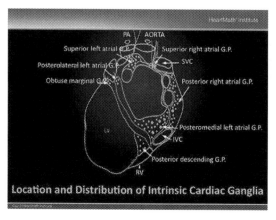

Image courtesy of the HeartMath® Institute – www.heartmath.org

The HeartMath[4] Institute located in Boulder Creek California has been performing groundbreaking studies that reveal the true nature of the human heart. The primary discovery was of the "heart brain," or "little brain in the heart". Ganglia, groups of nerve cells that exist outside the brain and spinal cord, have been identified in the heart. These highly specialized neurons do more than regulate heartbeats. In 1994, after extensive research, A.J. Armour introduced the concept of the functional 'heart brain'. His work revealed that the heart has a multifaceted intrinsic nervous system that is adequately sophisticated to qualify as a 'little brain' in its own right. The heart's brain is a complex network of various neurons, neurotransmitters, proteins and support cells similar to those found in the brain proper. Its elaborate circuitry enables it to act independently of the cranial brain—to learn, remember, and even feel and sense. The heart's nervous system contains around 40,000 neurons, called sensory neurites. Information from the heart - including feeling sensations - is sent to the brain through nerve pathways which enter the brain at the area of the medulla, and cascade up into the higher centers of the brain, where they may influence perception, decision making and other cognitive processes.

---

[4] Visit www.heartmath.org for up-to-date research projects and findings.

The brain responds to information from the heart by releasing what it deems the appropriate chemicals and hormones throughout the body.

It was discovered in 1983 that the heart also has the ability to release hormones to the body without the brain's assistance. Some of those identified include: atrial natriuretic factor (ANF), which can affect blood vessels, the adrenal gland, the kidneys, and regulatory centers in the brain; noradrenaline and dopamine neurotransmitters once thought to be produced only by neurons in the brain; and it was more recently discovered that the heart also secretes oxytocin, commonly referred to as the "love" hormone. In addition to its functions in childbirth and lactation, recent evidence indicates that this hormone is also involved in cognition, tolerance, adaptation, complex sexual and maternal behaviors, learning social cues and the establishment of enduring pair bonds. Concentrations of oxytocin in the heart were found to be as high as those found in the brain.

Numerous peer reviewed experiments evaluated subjects by evoking certain emotions then testing for specific chemical and hormonal responses. When the subject is stressed, agitated, or afraid, the brain kicks into "fight or flight" mode, releasing increased levels of adrenaline and cortisol into the bloodstream. This is helpful for the short term if the individual actually does have to fight or run fast, but not when experienced for hours a day, day after day. Our health suffers from the constant overload of stressful, negative emotions churning in our guts, manifesting in our hearts, resulting in our brains triggering a biological response that burdens our bodies with unnecessary, harmful agents.

But they also found the reverse to be true. When the test subjects were experiencing peace and calm, joy, gratitude, appreciation, and compassion, the signal sent to the brain by the heart resulted in boosted immune systems and the deliverance of anti-aging properties. There is actually a science of compassion that has affirmed the fact that when people engage in an activity that helps others endorphins are released causing them to be happier and healthier.

The term "coherence" is often used for the optimum frequency at which the heart and brain communicate to improve our health and well-being. Interestingly enough, that occurs when we are relaxed, at peace, with our thoughts and emotions focused on feelings of joy, gratitude, appreciation, compassion, or love—the very feelings that ingenuous spirituality encourages us to embody. *Finally, brothers and sisters, whatever is true, whatever is noble, whatever is right, whatever is pure, whatever is lovely, whatever is admirable—if anything is excellent or praiseworthy— think about such things.* (Philippians 4:8, NIV) *A cheerful heart is good medicine, but a crushed spirit dries up the bones.* (Proverbs 7:22, NIV) *In everything give thanks: for this is the will of God in Christ Jesus concerning you.* (1 Thessalonians 5:18) *It is good to praise the Lord and make music to your name, O Most High.* (Psalms 92:1, NIV) *Give thanks to the Lord, for he is good; his love endures forever.* (Psalms 106:1, NIV) *Enter his gates with thanksgiving and his courts with praise; give thanks to him and praise his name.* (Psalms 100:4, NIV) *But the fruit of the Spirit is love, joy, peace, long-suffering, gentleness, goodness, faith, meekness, temperance: against such there is no law.* (Galatians 5:22-23, NIV) *For the kingdom of God is not a matter of eating and drinking, but of righteousness, peace and joy in the Holy Spirit.* (Romans 14:17, NIV) *Turn from evil and do good; seek peace and pursue it.* (Psalms 34:14, NIV) *"Peace I leave with you; my peace I give you. I do not give to you as the world gives. Do not let your hearts be troubled and do not be afraid."* (John 14:27, NIV) *"I have told you these things, so that in me you may have peace. In this world you will have trouble. But take heart! I have overcome the world."* (John 16:33, NIV) *Therefore, as God's chosen people, holy and dearly loved, clothe yourselves with compassion, kindness, humility, gentleness and patience.* (Colossians 3:12, NIV) *Be kind and compassionate to one another, forgiving each other, just as in Christ God forgave you.* (Ephesians 4:32, NIV) *Do not be anxious about anything, but in every situation, by prayer and petition, with thanksgiving, present your requests to God.* (Philippians 4:6, NIV)

Jesus taught his followers not to worry or be anxious and stressed out because he knew how God made us to work; he knew that although the temptation to worry pounds on the door of our hearts, it is bad for us and we should simply trust God rather than fear circumstances.

> *25 "Therefore I tell you, do not worry about your life, what you will eat or drink; or about your body, what you will wear. Is not life more than food, and the body more than clothes? 26 Look at the birds of the air; they do not sow or reap or store*

away in barns, and yet your heavenly Father feeds them. Are you not much more valuable than they? 27 Can any one of you by worrying add a single hour to your life?

28 "And why do you worry about clothes? See how the flowers of the field grow. They do not labor or spin. 29 Yet I tell you that not even Solomon in all his splendor was dressed like one of these. 30 If that is how God clothes the grass of the field, which is here today and tomorrow is thrown into the fire, will he not much more clothe you—you of little faith? 31 So do not worry, saying, 'What shall we eat?' or 'What shall we drink?' or 'What shall we wear?' 32 For the pagans run after all these things, and your heavenly Father knows that you need them. 33 But seek first his kingdom and his righteousness, and all these things will be given to you as well. 34 Therefore do not worry about tomorrow, for tomorrow will worry about itself. Each day has enough trouble of its own. (Matthew 6: 25-34, NIV)

The Judaea-Christian faiths are not the only ones that teach us to honor these feelings in our hearts for the betterment of ourselves and mankind in general. The name "Islam" is derived from a word meaning "peace" in Arabic. Verses from the Quran are similar to those above: *"O You who believe! Enter absolutely into peace."* (Holy Quran: 2, 208) *"… Anyone who is grateful does so to the profit of his own soul…"* (Surah Al-Luqman 31:12) The word "compassion" is the most frequently occurring word in the Quran. Each of its 114 chapters, with the exception of the 9th, begins with the invocation "in the name of God, the Compassionate, the Merciful…" Recognized teachers of the faith have emphasized the importance of love, compassion, and the human heart. *"Love cannot be contained within our speaking or listening. Love is an ocean whose depths cannot be plumbed."* (Sufi writer Rumi, 1207) *"The Temple which contains Me (Allah) is in your heart." "The mystery of the Divine Essence is no other than the Temple of the heart, and it is around the heart that the spiritual pilgrim circumambulates."* (Tarjuman al-ashwaq)

The Buddhist tradition is perhaps the most clearly associated with non-violence and peace; peace, both internal and external, is the central message and discipline of the belief-system. Loving-kindness, compassion, appreciative joy, and a particular form of equanimity are the four kinds of love taught and encouraged in classic Buddhist teachings and they are four qualities of heart that reside within everyone, at least as potentials. While in the west we are taught to be grateful for blessings or good fortune, Buddhism teaches us to be grateful, period. Gratitude is to be cultivated as a habit or attitude of mind not dependent on conditions. Of joy, Buddha said, "Thousands of candles can be lighted from a single candle, and the life of the candle will not be shortened. Happiness never decreases by being shared," and, "We are shaped by our thoughts; we become what we think. When the mind is pure, joy follows like a shadow that never leaves." Compassion is also a central theme in Buddhism; Buddha taught that to gain enlightenment, one must develop two primary qualities—wisdom and compassion.

So we now know that when the Bible and other spiritual texts and teachings instruct us to feel thankfulness, joy, peace, appreciation, love and compassion, there is a very practical reason to do so—that is how the Creator made us! These are the feelings which most magnify the proper coherence between our heart and brain that cause us to be healthier, happier, and live longer. In addition to reducing stress and its effects, research has shown that achieving heart-brain coherence improves memory, boosts creativity and problem solving, and improves students' test scores. We tend to think that meditation requires twenty or thirty minutes a day, and that is a good target to set. Ideally we should develop a habit of keeping our hearts in a state of peace and harmony for most of our waking hours. But studies at the HeartMath Institute have documented that cortisol levels can decrease as much as 23 percent, and levels of DHEA, a life-affirming precursor to other vital hormones in the body, can increase 100 percent if we spend as little as three minutes using focused techniques designed to produce coherence!

We have learned that the heart performs many more extraordinary functions than science once knew and that it truly is the residence of our souls where emotions from the lower chakras meet thoughts from our brains to form feelings—feelings which in turn direct the health of our bodies and the directions of our lives. But there is another amazing phenomenon produced by our hearts. Many people who consider themselves educated scoff at the New Age notion of "auras" invisibly glowing around our bodies, sometimes in colors, that are rarely seen, even by people who believe in them. As it turns out, science has proved them right.

Have you ever walked into a room and could feel the tension when two or more people were having a heated disagreement? Perhaps you recall a person who "lit up the room" when she walked in, instantly uplifting the general mood. Why is it that we can even "feel" a "mood" in the room? The answer is one of the keys to who we as humans are. Both our brains and our hearts produce electric and magnetic fields that emanate from our bodies, but the heart's electric field is about ten times more powerful than the brain's and the heart's magnetic field is almost 100 times as powerful as the brain's.

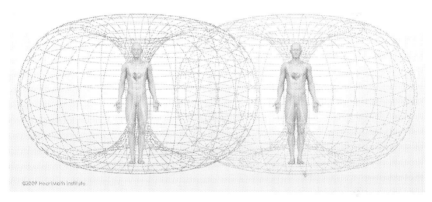

Heart generated magnetic fields
Image courtesy of the HeartMath® Institute – www.heartmath.org

The electromagnetic field generated by the heart extends a great distance from our core affecting those around us. The stronger the emotion being felt, the further away others can pick up on it. Scientifically, this explains why we can feel a mood in the room. Since humans have relied on spoken language to communicate for so many millennia, most of us have forgotten how to sense this exchange altogether, but our animal friends have not. Horses can easily pick up on the emotions of their riders, becoming jumpy or flighty if the rider is feeling afraid or insecure, but relaxing when the rider feels confident. Pets and wild animals alike can sense our emotions helping them determine if this person is a friend or a threat. A loyal companion gets excited when we are excited or in a good mood and likewise rubs against us to lend comfort when we are sad. They can easily comprehend the emotional signals that radiate through our body's electromagnetic field and respond with their own emotions which may cause us to become more uncertain or afraid, more happy and content, or sooth and comfort us. Some dogs are even sensitive enough to their human friends to know when they are getting sick or about to have a seizure.

The electro-magnetosphere of the sun and earth also interacts with that produced by our own bodies. We know that the weather, for example low barometric pressure vs. high pressure, can affect our minds, emotions, and bodies. Maybe you are that person who knows it is going to rain because your arthritic knee starts aching, or you get sleepy every time it rains. In general most people have uplifted moods when the sun is shining. These are examples of how electric and magnetic levels in the atmosphere affect our bodies; is it possible that the fields generated by our human hearts can likewise affect the weather? Researchers are beginning to explore this possibility.

We humans are all connected, both biologically going back to "Adam and Eve" and electromagnetically through the Field, the spiritual essence of God that exists in and between all things. But we are just now beginning to understand that we are also a part of everything in creation, and they are likewise connected to us. Studies at the HeartMath Institute have determined that trees and even the ground gives off electric and magnetic pulses[5]. Trees have a surprisingly complex range of electrical activity and rhythms. They clearly have circadian rhythms and other slower rhythms as well as faster ones. They are coupled in part to electrical potentials that researchers see waxing and waning with the sun and moon's gravitational pull on the earth. This shows that they, too, are connected to us through the electromagnetic field.

God is spirit, and his worshipers must worship in the Spirit and in truth. (John 4:24, NIV)

What is worship? In many Christian churches praise and worship are

---

[5] https://www.heartmath.org/research/featured-research/

lumped together and almost equated with the singing of spiritual songs. Music is a powerful language that transcends spoken tongues and can move us in inexplicable ways. It has played a part in organized worship for as far back as religions have been recorded and for a very good reason. In order to be performed properly, the musician must involve his mind, body, and emotion, bringing all three aspects of the person together focused on the same task at the same time. The mind is required to coordinate with the body to physically play the prescribed notes on the instrument with any level of proficiency, but any musician worth her salt understands that all the skill in the world is useless without the emotional aspect, without inserting feeling into the piece. Therefore, the mind, body, and emotion are all required to produce beautiful and meaningful music. Music often then becomes the means by which to create the proper feeling, the requisite atmosphere for worship to occur, but the music by itself is not worship.

Two of the most important contributions that the Pentecostal and Charismatic movements have made to Western spiritual traditions are the emphasis on emotion and bodily participation in worship. A mere intellectual exercise such as reciting words and rituals, even thinking correct doctrinal thoughts is not worship. Our feelings and emotions must be involved, or the participant is simply going through the motions. *Love the Lord your God with all your heart and with all your soul and with all your mind and with all your strength.* (Mark 12:30, NIV) Pair that with the earlier verse's "spirit and truth" and we see that using the mind alone is not sufficient. We must engage our feelings and emotions, and yes, our bodies (strength referring to the body). We have a mouth with which to sing or chant, hands to clap, arms to raise, body to sway, legs to dance, and feet to tap. "But we don't so that in our church; that makes me uncomfortable." It made people uncomfortable when King David laid aside his crown and robes and danced in the street to celebrate his God, but being a "man after God's own heart" he understood this principle. It may be out of place and disruptive for you to dance in the isle at your establishment, but I'm sure it would be ok for you to "make a joyful noise unto the Lord." Besides, worship is certainly not limited to church services; sadly, it rarely happens within them… everyone going through the motions but never achieving the goal.

As a worship team member and worship leader of several churches of varying denominations, I can testify that it is not the style of music or even the outward exuberance of the participants that makes the difference. I have been a part of contemporary, charismatic services where God's presence was so tangible you could swim in it, and I have been in services where the same songs were sung with the same instruments playing and absolutely nothing–dead as the proverbial doornail. I have likewise been in a church with traditional organ music or at a symphony concert and felt the elation of communing with the Almighty. It doesn't matter if it is Eastern music or Western music, classical, traditionally, Gospel, hymns, or praise choruses–the style of music is no more than a preference agreed upon by the membership. The purpose of the music is to create the feeling of God's presence in the room and the only way to achieve that is for the singers and musicians to actually be worshiping themselves.

Some leaders believe that everything must be rehearsed, practiced, perfected, and performed precisely before the congregation; others claim that is too rigid. Instead they prefer to "wing it," and be spontaneous. Both of these practices are flawed, but combining elements of each creates a meaningful balance. The worship leader who hasn't planned songs in advance has to think about what to sing or play next and therefore isn't able to focus his attention on worshiping. Leaving the worship team members clueless as to what comes next also creates at least some level of uncertainty or anxiety. Additionally, poor performance due to lack of rehearsal detracts as the people hear the mistakes, directing their focus away from worshiping. But the one who leaves no room for spontaneity may well squelch the inspiration of the Holy Spirit. He may also have his musicians concentrating so hard on a good performance that they cannot experience worship themselves. Practice, yes, that is essential. The more prepared you are, the easier it becomes to be in the moment. Those who fail to practice, do not honor God with their talents and responsibilities. *Sing to him a new song; play skillfully and shout for joy.* (Psalm 33:3) But the main problem I have encountered with both style of directors is that they miss the point of what they are doing altogether; worship leaders–whether the organist, pianist, drummer, guitarist, orchestra member, choir singer, a hand bell ringer, or director–must lead by actually engaging in worship themselves! We must employ our minds, hearts, souls, and bodies not only in producing good music, but in creating the feeling of the presence of

God in our own hearts while we play and sing, so that feeling may extend outward through our magnetic fields to the pulpit and dais and on to the congregation.

One of the most profound worship experiences I have participated in occurred quite spontaneously while I was attending a music conference at Montreat, North Carolina. One of our classes had just ended and several of us musicians gathered around a piano complete with pianist. There was a violin, a flute, perhaps a cello and clarinet, and me on French horn. Someone suggested we have a jam session. Now all the participants were accomplished musicians who had spent decades perfecting our talents, so the rehearsing part had been well covered. We asked the pianist to begin playing a chord progression of her choice and one by one we instinctively joined in, taking turns creating a melody over the chords while the others devised harmonies and background. We must have all been doing what I was doing, focusing on creating a beautiful, unique "new song" unto the Lord, an expression of love and adoration, appreciation and thanksgiving, because in a matter of moments the feeling arose. We continued the improvisation for a good ten minutes or longer, the small classroom flooded with the tangible presence of I Am, and each one of us was wowed. There were many fine performances during services at the conference and other instances where God's presence was felt, but none as powerful as that small group of musicians doing what we do.

Everything involved should be for the purpose of prompting the people's hearts toward worship—from beautiful architecture and art, stained glass windows, and banners to prayers, readings, candles, rituals, drama, dance, and music. It is all there to help the congregation feel the presence of God, but worship does not require a building, service, or any of the afore mentioned aides. Worship isn't a rite or a ceremony and transcends all religious designations and doctrines; it does not require a priest or minister or any religious trappings. Worship is something we feel in our hearts... or we don't. When thoughts of how awesome and magnificent is Yahweh, how great is His love and compassion toward us, thoughts of praise and thanksgiving for all He has created and done are combined with the emotion of love, the result is a feeling we call worship. It must come from the heart or it is but a pretense. *The Lord says: "These people come near to me with their mouth and honor me with their lips, but their hearts are far from me. Their worship of me is based on merely human rules they have been taught.* (Isaiah 29:13, NIV)

There is nothing wrong with reciting creeds, corporate prayer, scripture readings, and singing songs; all of these help to focus our thoughts in the right direction. The problem is that Western culture elevates the mind and intellect at the expense of emotion. Sometimes our men are even taught to push down or ignore their emotions, but this is to our detriment. Turning our thoughts and words toward praising and thanking God is required for worship, but so is bringing our emotion of love and the feelings of our heart into the experience. It is the combining of all three that create the encounter; the feeling *is* the worship.

God's presence is everywhere, all the time, but we don't feel it all the time. That is what the music is for – to create the feeling. *Enter his gates with thanksgiving and his courts with praise; give thanks to him and praise his name.* (Psalms 100:4, NIV) *But You are holy, Enthroned in the praises of Israel.* (Psalms 22:3, NLT) God is everywhere, yet we are told that He inhabits the praises of His people. There is a scientific reason for that. Even though the Divine Holy Spirit dwells in every rock, tree, river, and person, in worship we experience His presence in a more personal way. When our thoughts, feelings, and emotions become as one, focused on the goodness of God, we are able to communicate with His invisible Greatness through the coherence of our hearts. Those waves of electricity and magnetism emanating from our hearts just as the Creator intended are our true means of connecting with the Almighty. Yes, our brains do produce waves as well, and yes God can hear our thoughts and we can communicate with him through our brains, but the heart's field is much greater, therefore produces a stronger conduit. It is only with the heart that we can feel the presence of Elohim, and in that presence give to Him our love, praise, honor, thanks, and adoration; it is in that presence that He expresses His love toward us with comfort and compassion, imparts to us wisdom and revelation, bestows joy and peace, and transforms us from glory to glory.

While we can worship at home, at the beach or lake, in our cars, or anywhere, there is a potential for great power in groups. Just think–you are standing in the congregation with your thoughts, feelings, and emotions focused on grateful praise and adoration, pumping out an aura of positive energy from your heart, a field that extends into the space the person next to you occupies, when she begins to worship, projecting her field, and is joined by the man next to her and the guy across the aisle. Imagine dozens, hundreds, or even thousands of people in the room experience the same feelings of genuine worship creating a huge electromagnetic field of positive energy, all those hearts resonating at the same frequency of coherence. The cloud of worship vibe spreads beyond the room into the nursery, children's space, even out onto the sidewalk and street; people passing by can feel the peace and love emanating beyond the walls. It is in this atmosphere of worship that wounds can be healed, forgiveness given and received, reconciliation transpire, bodies, minds, and spirits healed, transformations take place. The power of the worship experience is multiplied and therefore so are the results.

Studies at the HeartMath Institute have determined that when groups of people practice heart coherence at the same time, even if they are not in proximity to each other, their heart-waves connect. This study, titled the Global HRV Synchronization study, showed that human heart rhythms of participants synchronized with other participants, even in some cases in which the participants were located hundreds of miles apart. This indicated that the participants were all synchronized to an external signal in Earth's magnetic field environment.

The gathering together of spiritual, loving people to worship, fellowship, or volunteer in service projects is a good, worthwhile use of our time–unless it is killing our spirits. We must ask ourselves several critical questions: 1) Why do I attend? If the answer is to please my loved one, to set a good example for the kids, to look good in front of the community, to fulfill an obligation, because I think I have to, so God won't be mad at me, to win the pastor's approval, or any other often used reason, then you may as well stay home. Unless the answer is "because I love God and have a deep desire to worship Him and demonstrate love towards others both in and outside of our fellowship" then you are just going through the motions. 2) How often do I really feel the unmistakable presence of God in my worship service? You may not every week, or even on a regular basis, but if the answer is seldom to never, then you may want to consider one of two reasons–either *you* aren't actually entering into worship, or *no one else there* is actually entering into worship that is spirit and truth. And if everyone present is just going through the motions, you may want to consider finding another place of worship. 3) If your leader talks more about who and what God hates than who and what God loves, if he/she discourages your independent study, thought, and interpretation of scriptures, if he/she excels at telling everyone what they ought to do, say, think, and especially how to vote, if he/she places strong emphasis on members giving money to their organization, if more of that money is spent on projects to benefit the membership than the poor, then at best you could be a member of a mere social club and at worst a cult led by a dangerous demagogue, regardless of what label hangs over the door. Churches, mosques, temples, and synagogues can and do much to bring people closer to God and to extend His love into the world; then again, many of them simply don't. Examine yourself and your place of worship to determine if it is truly where you belong.

> 5 *"And when you pray, do not be like the hypocrites, for they love to pray standing in the synagogues and on the street corners to be seen by others. Truly I tell you, they have received their reward in full. 6 But when you pray, go into your room, close the door and pray to your Father, who is unseen. Then your Father, who sees what is done in secret, will reward you. 7 And when you pray, do not keep on babbling like pagans, for they think they will be heard because of their many words. 8 Do not be like them, for your Father knows what you need before you ask him.* (Matthew 6:5-8, NIV)

What is Prayer? Worship and prayer, both being forms of communication with Adonai, are two aspects of the same encounter, like flips sides of a single coin. There is no single right or wrong way to pray, and prayer comes in several modes. There is the informal colloquial prayer, or a conversation with God. Also popular is petitionary prayer which is asking for something whether it is for your own needs or the needs and wellbeing of others. There are ritualistic prayers, a written or recited prayer such as may be found in a prayer book, a frequently used blessing for a meal, or words taught to a child such as, "God is Great, God is Good," or "Now I lay me down to sleep." The last commonly identified method of prayer is meditation; some people consider meditation to be apart from prayer while others view it as a type of prayer. These are all legitimate traditions of praying and can be very meaningful, but there is a method of prayer spoken of in scriptures and practiced by people of varying faiths that goes beyond these. Gregg Braden called it "the lost mode of prayer."

Several Biblical passages reference this method of prayer. Let me begin by explaining that this is "heart prayer," rather than "head prayer." *The effectual fervent prayer of a righteous man availeth much.* (James 5:16) True prayer is not words, or not just words; to be effectual, it must originate from the heart.

> *9 To some who were confident of their own righteousness and looked down on everyone else, Jesus told this parable: 10 "Two men went up to the temple to pray, one a Pharisee and the other a tax collector. 11 The Pharisee stood by himself and prayed: 'God, I thank you that I am not like other people— robbers, evildoers, adulterers—or even like this tax collector. 12 I fast twice a week and give a tenth of all I get.' 13 But the tax collector stood at a distance. He would not even look up to heaven, but beat his breast and said, 'God, have mercy on me, a sinner.' 14 I tell you that this man, rather than the other, went home justified before God. For all those who exalt themselves will be humbled, and those who humble themselves will be exalted."* (Luke 18:9-14, NIV)

In this passage Jesus makes it clear that the religious Pharisee with his eloquent words did not engage in true prayer while the non-religious tax collector whose cry came from his heart was heard by God. Words alone are meaningless to the Father, as 1 Corinthians 13:1 states, *"If I speak in the tongues of men or of angels, but do not have love, I am only a resounding gong or a clanging cymbal."* (NIV) The emotion of love must join with our words or thoughts to create a feeling in our hearts that then communicates with the Mind of God through the Field.

But what sets this "lost mode of prayer" apart from even the effectual fervent prayer is the belief that the prayer has already been answered. *"If you believe, you will receive whatever you ask for in prayer."* (Matthew 21:22, NIV) *Therefore I tell you, whatever you ask for in prayer, believe that you have received it, and it will be yours.* (Mark 11:24, NIV) In John 16:23-24 Jesus tells us, *23 "In that day you will no longer ask me anything. Very truly I tell you, my Father will give you whatever you ask in my name. 24 Until now you have not asked for anything in my name. Ask and you will receive, and your joy will be complete."* (NIV) However, this passage, like many others, was edited and condensed by the Council of Nicaea when they canonized the Holy Bible. The original text in Aramaic with a direct translation reads, *"All things that you ask straightly, directly from inside my name you will be given. So far you've not done this. Ask without hidden motive and be surrounded by your answer. Be enveloped by what you desire that your gladness be full."*

As we examine these verses, there are two keys ideas to define: "believe" and "in Jesus name." A belief must occur in the heart where an idea formed in the mind is charged with the emotion of love (or fear if it is a negative belief) creating a feeling of confidence that the mind's idea is truth. Believing is very similar to having faith. Hebrews 11:1 instructs us, *Now faith is the substance of things hoped for, the evidence of things not seen.* Many people say they have faith without actually even understanding what that means. Often times it is said that we must "take on faith" that which cannot be proven, but this passage sets a very high standard for faith. Believing something, having faith, is to live your life as if that thing has already been proven. Faith is substance and evidence, not wishing or hoping. Substance is tangible; evidence is proof. Belief is not an intellectual exercise nor is it an emotional "wishy-hopey" gamble; it is confident knowledge of what is, even if you haven't seen it or it hasn't happened yet. It must include thought and emotion, manifest in heart coherence which feels that peace that passes understanding. Jesus taught in Matthew 17:20, *"Truly I tell you, if you have faith as small as a mustard seed, you can say to this mountain, 'Move from here to there,' and it will move. Nothing will be impossible for you."* (NIV) And again in Mark 11:23, *"Truly I tell you, if anyone says to this mountain, 'Go, throw yourself into the sea,' and does not doubt in their heart but believes that what they say will happen, it will be done for them."* (NIV) Some people have had mountain-moving experiences, but overall that seems to be rare. I think one of our stumbling blocks is that we truly do not understand what it is to "believe in our hearts."

For centuries, and even in most churches today, people simply do not comprehend what it means to "pray in Jesus' name." Pastors and lay people of all denominations have been taught to tack on the verbal phrase, "in Jesus' name," or "in the name of the Father, Son, and Holy Spirit," to a prayer to give it legitimacy. However, we have already established that prayer is not words; therefore to simply say, "in Jesus' name" is meaningless. If you recall, in part two of this manuscript I showed you how formal logic dictates that if God is love and Jesus is God, then Jesus is love. To pray from "inside his name" is to pray in love! The emotion of love must fuel the prayer even as thoughts guide its direction. This love can be applied to any mode of prayer, even prayers read from a book or order of service paper. It can be applied to colloquial prayer or prayers of petition. It can power your meditation even as it powers your faith. Love is the engine that propels the effectual fervent prayer; indeed, without the love motivator, a prayer is impotent.

With those things in mind, let's look back at the unabridged version of John 16:23-24. First the prayer must come from inside a place of love, "inside my name." Next are two keys: "Ask without hidden motive." Why are you initiating this prayer? What is your reason, your motivation? Examine your motives to see that they are pure, unselfish, and without judgment. This doesn't mean you can't pray for your own needs and the desires of your heart; after all, Psalms 37:4 promises, *Take delight in the Lord, and he will give you the desires of your heart.* (NIV) But consider, if you will, a different interpretation of this verse. I don't believe it means that if we but find our joy in the Lord, he will give us whatever we want; I think it means if we find our joy in the Lord, he will place the desires we should have in our hearts–not that He will grant what we want, but that He will cause us to want the same things He wants, desires that are untainted, generous, lovely, and beneficial to all His creation.

Next, "be surrounded by your answer. Be enveloped by what you desire that your gladness be full." To be surrounded by and enveloped by is to feel the feeling that the prayer has already been answered. It is to grab hold of that substance and evidence of faith; it is to believe you have what you prayed for even if you can't see it with your eyes. In his book, "The Divine Matrix," Gregg Braden relates a story of a time he visited a Native American friend during a time of severe drought. His friend was going up onto a special hill to pray for rain and Gregg asked to go with him. When they arrived, his friend took off his shoes, closed his eyes, and lifted his face and hands toward the sky. He stood there for a few minutes, then said, "Lets' go have lunch now," and put his shoes back on. Gregg had questions. "But I thought we were going to pray for rain." His friend answered, "If we pray *for* rain we acknowledge that there is no rain and the drought would continue." "Then what were you doing?" Gregg asked. His friend explained, "I was feeling raindrops hitting my face and mud between my toes. I was smelling the scent of fresh rain and feeling my hands, arms, and clothes becoming wet. Then I gave thanks for the rain that we need so much." Gregg reported that night had the largest rain storm the area had experienced for months and it continued to rain all the next day.

In the Book of Thomas, saying 48, Jesus is quoted as teaching, *"If two make peace with one another in this one house, they will say to the mountain: Be removed, and it will be removed."* While some interpret this as meaning two people being in agreement, it is very likely that he was referring to thought and emotion. We know from other Biblical passages that Jesus often refers to the human body as a house or temple; the body is the "house" in which our spirit resides while on earth. It is probable that in this saying Jesus is instructing us how to pray a powerful prayer by lining up our thought and emotion in peace together to create a feeling that the prayer has in fact been answered. Then we can say to the mountain, "be moved" and it will be moved.

Again, when Gregg Braden visited the monastery in Tibet, he observed the monks in prayer. He asked them, "When I watch your prayers and hear the gongs and instruments and the chants and mantras that you use, what are you doing on the inside? What is going on in your minds and hearts?" The monk replied, "You have never seen our prayers because a prayer cannot be seen. The gongs, instruments, chants, and refrains you hear are not the prayers; we use them to create the feeling, and the feeling is the prayer."

"So," you may ask, "Has this worked for you?" Since the time I was first introduced to Gregg Braden's "The Lost Mode of Prayer," I have encountered three health challenges. The first was already in full swing when I read his book and I did attempt to put into practice what I was learning. Due to an old injury, the cartilage of my right knee had slowly been rubbing away until the point it was causing extreme pain and limiting my mobility. I went to see a sports medicine joint specialist and the x-rays clearly showed bone scraping bone in a spot where no knee padding remained. While they tried several non-surgical treatments, I began to spend twenty to thirty minutes a night in prayer and meditation attempting to heal the problem with mixed results. I was able to alleviate pain that way, but not to permanently solve the issue. I did, however, feel very positively about getting knee replacement surgery even though I was still in my forties. With an excellent surgeon, great hospital care, and a stringent physical therapy regiment, I was quickly back to 100%. But the story doesn't end there. In the first few years afterward, metal detectors beeped at my knee and I could feel the cold of the metal inside when out in below freezing temperatures. I have good reason to believe that new bone and cartilage have formed around the implant creating a completely repaired joint because metal detectors no longer beep and my knee and it no longer reacts to cold temperatures. It behaves exactly the same as my natural knee.

The second challenge arose when I went in for my yearly checkup and blood work and the doctor came back in the room to announce that I had diabetes. Immediately a fierce determination rose up in my spirit and the first thing to pop into my mind was, "Oh no I don't! There is no way, no how, that I am going to have diabetes!" This was not a denial of facts; I believed what the blood tests showed, but I was resolved to fighting and beating this diagnosis. My doctor put me on a diet and exercise program and gave me pills to take and I followed my regimen to the letter. After six months my blood sugar was lower, but not normal yet. Then I began to experiment with my diet. Everyone's body chemistry is a little different and what works for one person doesn't work for everyone. I tested different foods and discovered that rice and pasta (even the "healthy" brown rice and whole-wheat pasta) were what caused my blood sugar to spike, so I cut them out completely. Next check up by blood sugar was down but not normal yet. It was time to make a serious decision, one I realize not everyone has the luxury of making. I had figured out why my blood sugar got high in the first place – my overly stressful job. I had gotten so stressed at work that I started over eating junk foods as a comfort and had gained forty pounds. By this point I had lost much of the weight but my job stress level was going nowhere but up. So at fifty-four years old I changed careers and became an over-the-road truck driver. Stress practically vanished, I lost the rest of the weight I had gained, and over four years have doubled my salary – and my blood sugar returned to normal where it has stayed for these four years, even without medication of any kind. My doctor testifies that she has had other patients reverse their diabetes and even get off of insulin despite what some in the medical profession say; after-all, chronic illnesses are big money makers for pharmaceutical companies. So how does this example fit into prayer? Simple. Remember the six parameters I mentioned earlier: breath, nutrient, movement, thought, feeling, and emotion. Three are physical, outward necessities to good health and three are inward but just as relevant. To achieve success I had to apply the correct solution to all six parameters. Praying without the lifestyle changes is like asking for handouts when you are too lazy to work, but many people change their diet and never kick diabetes; there is great power in belief. I refused to believe I was stuck with this ailment and persisted in my belief that it would go. Can I now revert back to gorging out on junk food and letting myself be stressed? No; if I do my blood sugar will go back up, but then again that is the main reason diabetes is running amuck in our society. We simply cannot have our cake and eat it too.

The third challenge came along in the spring of 2016 when I started suffering from occasional bouts of extremely painful heartburn. In the past I had been diagnosed with gastric reflux and took pills for it, but that completely disappeared when I changed jobs and I hadn't needed an acid reducer in years. Wondering if it had come back to haunt me, I went to the doctor. An endoscopy uncovered the culprit to be a hiatal hernia. The doctor said sometimes they repair themselves, sometimes you are stuck with it for life, and an operation to repair it had about a 50/50 chance of permanent success. I decided to employ prayer and meditation to heal the hernia and avoid any large meals. After a few weeks my symptoms disappeared and have not returned. I have declared the hernia healed. No, I didn't go back to the doctor because I don't need to pay someone when I feel fine and there's nothing definitive they could do anyway except confirm it is gone or say it's still there but if it's not bothering you don't worry about it.

As you can see, I have experienced success in dealing with health issues through a combination of traditional medical treatments, diet, exercise, relaxation meditation, lifestyle changes, and prayer by which I see the resulting answer and believe it to be true. I do not suggest ignoring doctors, operations, or medicines because God gave us intelligence to discover and invent cures for our ailments and sometimes that is the best route to take. But I also do not put my faith in doctors, operations, or medicines because God also created our bodies with the ability to heal themselves, if we can just figure out how to do it. The truth is that we can participate in our own healing through our thoughts, feelings, and emotions along with nutrition, breathing, and movement, or we can inhibit our own recovery though negative thoughts, feelings, and emotions as well as by continuing in poor nutritional and exercise habits. I respect medical professionals, but I trust in the Divine Creator, Master of the Universe who indwells me and all living things and in the power He can give to us.

Thought prayers are real as God can sense our thoughts; heart prayers are fervent effectual prayers with far more potency. But in this fifth mode of prayer where the individual lines up in perfect agreement her thoughts and emotions to create a feeling in which she experiences life as if the prayer has already been answered–that is how we create our own reality. We must understand that while a prayer may include words, the words are not the prayer; the feeling is the prayer.

1 Thessalonians 5:16-18 instructs us to pray all the time. *16 Rejoice always, 17 pray continually, 18 give thanks in all circumstances; for this is God's will for you in Christ Jesus.* (NIV) "But I have to go to work, take care of my family, do practical things; I can't pray without ceasing!" While it is true that we cannot spend every waking hour engaged in deep, focused prayer, the surrounding verses explain what is meant. We can, with effort and practice, gear our hearts into harmonic coherence, tune them to God's frequency so to speak, while we go about our daily tasks. Some people refer to this as an "attitude of gratitude." The world bombards us with negativity from every direction so it is up to us to create peace in our own hearts without relying on any externals for our joy or affirmation. When we focus on peace, compassion, appreciation, love, and thankfulness with every breath we take in and let out, when our thoughts are directed toward the positive and our feelings powered by love, then we can achieve the Apostle Paul's directive in these verses, and in doing so through the interaction of our thoughts, feelings, and emotions remain in constant contact with the

Divine Spirit which is both within and without us, keeping the conduit of our hearts open, which results in our own mental, physical, and spiritual well-being.

> *"All transformation begins with an intense, burning desire to be transformed. You must want to be different and intend to be before you can begin to change yourself. Then you MUST MAKE YOUR FUTURE DREAM A PRESENT FACT."*

> *"You do this by assuming the feeling of your wish fulfilled. By desiring to be other than what you are, you can create an ideal of the person you want to be and assume that you are already that person. If this assumption is persisted in until it becomes your dominant feeling, the attainment of your ideal is inevitable."* –Neville Goddard

Our perception of ourselves and the world around us shapes our reality. I am not speaking of obvious delusions here, like becoming the next center for the Lakers or the new richest man in the world, but we tend to see what we look for. Jesus said, "Seek and you shall find," but many people mostly spend their time looking for the negative. If we expect failure, disappointments, bad luck, and everything to go wrong, it probably will. Likewise, if we are on the lookout for what is beautiful and kind, if we anticipate success, positive relationships, and good fortune that is what we will get. The fact is that everyone's car breaks down sometime, we all have at least one relationship go wrong, and at some point we all experience failure and disappointment; those are part of life. Any law enforcement agent will say that if there are twelve witnesses to a crime, you'll get twelve different versions of what happened. James McCrae said, "Reality is created by focus. Wherever we focus our perception, a personal experience takes shape. When we shift our perception, we will inevitably experience a different world." "What you see reflects your thinking, and your thinking but reflects the choice of what you want to see," from *A Course In Miracles*. Dale Carnegie wrote, "Two men looked out from prison bars; one saw the mud, the other saw stars." René Descartes is known for stating, "I think, therefore I am." In another sense, one could say, "I am who or what I think I am." The lens through which we view ourselves, others, and our circumstances to a large extent determines our own happiness, health, and prosperity. Let me share some stories, one frequently retold and the others from my own experience.

A reporter was writing a story about the differences in children from well-to-do homes and those living in poverty. He first visited an upper-middle income family. The big house was in perfect repair with a large, green lawn. In back was a swimming pool, jungle-gym set, and trampoline. Inside the immaculate house he observed nice furnishing, books and artwork. When he asked if he could speak with the child, the parents led him upstairs and showed him the door to their son's room. When he opened it, the reporter was amazed at the spacious chamber. Shelves held books, games, and toys of every description. He saw a big screen TV with several video game consoles attached. Sitting in the middle of the floor surrounded by cars, trucks, a train, and action figures galore was a red-faced boy of about eight or ten with his arms crossed over his chest and an angry scowl on his pudgy face. "What is wrong?" the reporter asked, to which the child spat out, "I'm bored; I don't have anything to do." Bewildered, the reporter left and traveled across town to the projects. There he spoke with a single mother outside her tiny, ramshackle house with the broken screen door. The yard was mostly dirt with some weeds thrown in for good measure. He was concerned about entering the residence as he feared the roof might collapse at any moment. When he asked to speak with the children, the mother showed him around back where a little boy and his sister were playing. He watched for a moment as they dug in the dirt with old, bent spoons. "What are you doing?" the reporter asked. Two beaming faces shone up at him. The boy answered enthusiastically, "We are digging a deep, deep hole, all the way to the center of the earth!" Then his sister chimed in, "And with the dirt that comes out of the hole, we are building a great, huge mountain all the way up to the sky!" The reporter shook his head as he walked away. Then it dawned on him: the child who had everything perceived that he had nothing, while the ones who had nothing lived as if they had everything.

When I was in my early thirties and my parents were pushing eighty, my father was chosen to be ordained a "life deacon" by the First Baptist Church. This was an honor bestowed upon those who had faithfully served as deacon for many prior years and were now in the winter of their lives. I made a point of being present for the informal ceremony in the Fellowship Hall on a Wednesday evening. When my father stood at the lectern to give his personal testimony, the first words out of his mouth were, "It was not always easy growing up or living with a handicap..." and I didn't hear another word. I was completely stunned! Never in my thirty-plus years had the thought ever even hovered near my mind that my Daddy, the strongest, kindest, most honorable man I had ever known, could possibly be *handicapped*! Sure, I knew the story behind his foot, how when he was a little boy a door had closed on it breaking his ankle, how because they were a poor family living in the Mississippi Delta it never got set properly, how it developed an infection that was dormant most of the time but flared up every now and again. I knew about how when everyone was being drafted for World War II he was excused because he didn't pass the army physical requirements. I considered that a tremendous blessing; while thousands of his peers were being killed on the beaches of Normandy, he was back home marrying my mother. So he had to wear a special shoe and sometimes needed to soak his foot and wear bunion pads, big deal; he didn't complain about it. Sure, he never played basketball or baseball, but what did that matter? Daddy liked hunting and fishing. Maybe he couldn't run, but why would he need to? He was an engineer who worked with his brain and was an excellent provider for our family financially and in every way. I remember considering for the very first time how others may have looked at my father, with his club foot and uneven shoulders because one leg was shorter than the other; did other people see him somehow as *disabled*? From my earliest recollection to the day my father passed into eternity that was the only occasion when I heard him utter the words "handicapped" or "disabled" in reference to himself, and I lived my entire life until that point without ever once seeing my big, strong, capable Daddy as even the slightest bit handicapped, because in my perception of reality, he simply wasn't.

On an occasion while I was still in high school, my mother (whose fatal flaw was that she worried about everything) looked up at me with distressed brown eyes and asked, very seriously, "Are you embarrassed of me?" Puzzled, and wondering whatever she could have done that would embarrass me, I replied emphatically, "No, why should I be?" She went on to say because she wasn't young, pretty, and energetic like the other mothers, because she was the age of all my friends' grandmothers, and a string of similar nonsense. I remember thinking, *why would anyone be embarrassed of their parents' age? I'm glad I have older, more experienced parents who made all their mistakes on my big sister, and now my Daddy is at the top of his career making good money instead of just getting by.* She must have known people in her youth that would have been petty about that kind of thing, but I simply could not conceive of any other attitude about my parents apart from love and appreciation.

It isn't what we are dealt in life that matters, rather how we perceive and respond to our circumstances. "Old parents, what a bummer," someone may complain. "Oh, poor me; I can't accomplish anything in life because I have a hurt foot," another may bemoan. Maybe some people use their inadequacies as an excuse for why they never live up to their potential, but in most cases I believe the real culprit is fear, or perhaps a measure of laziness. They are afraid they won't succeed if they really try – or they're afraid they will succeed and people's expectations of them will rise. But is there any sin greater than wasted potential? *Let the weak say, I am strong.* (Joel 3:10) *But He said to me, "My grace is sufficient for you, for my power is made perfect in weakness."* (2 Corinthians 12:9, NIV) *Sorrowful, yet always rejoicing; poor, yet making many rich; having nothing, and yet possessing everything.* (2 Corinthians 6:10, NIV) *See, I am doing a new thing! Now it springs up; do you not perceive it? I am making a way in the wilderness and streams in the wasteland.* (Isaiah 43:19, NIV) *"The garden of the world has no limits, except in your mind."* Rumi

I was taught that every person is composed of his biology (genetics), environment (where and how he was raised), and will (decisions he makes for himself) in pretty much equal parts. But the older and more experienced I become, the more I learn and grow, the more I see that the third component far overshadows the other two. True, there are some things about our biology that we can't change. We can't will ourselves to be taller or shorter, have a different skin color or IQ, but studies have concluded that we *can* change our DNA!

The science of epigenetics (the study of how environmental factors outside of DNA influence changes in gene expression) have proved that stem cells and DNA can possibly be altered. This can be done through magnetic fields, heart coherence, positive mental states, and intention. Dr. Ventura of the University of Bologna, Italy has carried out his own research which showed that the DNA of stem cells can be altered using magnetic field frequencies. Researchers have also carried out experiments that showed the DNA of subjects who were experiencing anxiety, anger, and various negative emotions became tightly wound corkscrews while the DNA of subjects who sensed peace, joy, and different positive emotions became visibly relaxed and loose. Long before the discovery of DNA the expressions of being "wound up" or "loose" came into our vocabulary to describe feelings of stress or relaxation; now we know that is exactly what happens to our DNA strands when we experience those feelings.

The research hasn't ended there. Genetic determinists would have us believe that certain people are born with an addictive gene, a cancer gene, an allergy gene, a "fat" gene, and there is simply nothing you can do about it; you are a victim of genetics. But research has disproved the notion that "there is nothing you can do about it." While the sequence of DNA may not be affected by your environment, the way genes work—called gene expression—can. Environmental factors such as food, drugs, or exposure to toxins can cause epigenetic changes by altering the way molecules bind to DNA or changing the structure of proteins that DNA wraps around. Additionally, internal stimuli such as excessive stress or heart coherence can modify our genes. These structural variations can result in slight changes in gene activity; they also can produce more dramatic changes by switching genes on when they should be off or vice versa. The "addiction gene" is a documented example. Some people have affectively "shut off" their addiction gene with a combination of nutritional and emotional support along with lifestyle changes that eliminate the desire to engage in the addictive behavior.

Diet is another factor that can affect our DNA. Nutritionists have long known that "you are what you eat" is not just an expression. Recent studies suggest that what you eat affects you and sometimes even your children and grandchildren. A person's diet is an important source of epigenetic signals, and scientists are now investigating how eating habits modify gene expression in adults and their offspring. Understanding that relationship could help researchers identify nutritional elements that might help prevent or treat diseases such as obesity, diabetes, coronary artery disease, cancer and Alzheimer's. Organizations such as Nestlé, EpiGen Global Research Consortium, the German Research Center for Environmental Health, McGill University Medical School in Montreal, Karolinska Institute in Sweden, and New York's Mount Sinai hospital are currently conducting research into how nutrition, exercise, mood, and diverse environmental factors including, but not limited to, plastic, electromagnetic currents, and hazardous materials alter our genes, changes that may be passed down to our descendants.

Some environmental elements are within our control, but for the three dynamics that determine who we are, we will consider those beyond our control–how and where we were raised as children. We could not control how wealthy or poor our parents were, how many children were in the home, what kind of care and attention we received, what food was given to us, or what schools we were sent to. I have heard of studies done to determine a person's future success based on the neighborhood into which he was born, and while correlations obviously exist, they are by no means a determining factor. Certainly there is evidence that poverty breeds poverty, that children from one neighborhood are more likely to die young, become addicts, land in prison, etc. while those in the affluent part of town more likely to go to college, acquire good jobs, and become "contributing members of society." Conversely, sometimes the poor child becomes a doctor, lawyer, or pastor while the rich child squanders his good fortune and ends up the one dead, in prison, or living a miserable, self-centered life. Surely the child from a loving home with parents who treated her with respect and did their best to "train her up in the way she should go" has a boost that the child who was beaten, abused, or neglected never had, but that does not always ensure that child's future success or failure.

As a public school teacher I saw plenty of teenage girls with babies just as their mothers had been, plenty who dropped out of school or got handed from one boyfriend to the next; but I also taught students who raised themselves out of that subculture, got their education, waited for marriage to start a family. I had students who put themselves in jail from drugs, theft, assault, and in one case murder, and they weren't all from disadvantaged families. A child's environment can hold him back or launch him forward, but ultimately it is the third factor in who we are that is the primary determinate of our destinies: our will.

I remember having discussions with my sister about which played a larger role in shaping our lives, genetics or environment; I now can say with absolute certainty that it is neither. The choices we make, our own God-given free will makes all the difference. In his poem *Invictus*, William Ernest Henley wrote the often quoted phrase, "I am the master of my fate, I am the captain of my soul." The truth is we get to decide who we are! We choose to believe we are merely a result of chance or the beloved creation of a Higher Power. We choose to be a victim of all the bad in the world or an overcomer. We choose to live in fear, bitterness, unhappiness, and defeat or to live in love, forgiveness, and joyful appreciation of all the beauty that surrounds. There is no one to blame, no excuse to be made. *"So then, each of us will give an account of ourselves to God."* (Romans 14:12, NIV) *"But if serving the Lord seems undesirable to you, then choose for yourselves this day whom you will serve, whether the gods your ancestors served beyond the Euphrates, or the gods of the Amorites, in whose land you are living. But as for me and my household, we will serve the Lord."* (Joshua 24:15, NIV) *This day I call the heavens and the earth as witnesses against you that I have set before you life and death, blessings and curses. Now choose life, so that you and your children may live and that you may love the Lord your God, listen to his voice, and hold fast to him. For the Lord is your life, and he will give you many years in the land he swore to give to your fathers, Abraham, Isaac and Jacob.* (Deuteronomy 30:19-20, NIV)

There are three questions of vital importance that every human being should ask themselves; sadly, most of us are so busy just trying to get through the day that we never stop to reflect on our lives. 1) "Who am I?" Not what do I do for my job or how am I related to other people, but what is my character, my strengths and weaknesses. Is my life directed more by fear or by love? 2) "Who do I want to be?" Not a pro-athlete or movie star, but what kind of person do I want to be? What are my personal aspirations, potentials to develop, faults to overcome, characteristics to foster? 3) "What's stopping me from becoming that person?" Maybe some of us examine who we are and perhaps a few even consider who we wish to become, but then come the rationalizations, why it isn't possible, the reasons it will never happen for us. Some people are prevented from becoming because of wrong motives such as greed, lust, and gluttony, or simply by apathy, but for most people it is fear. Low self-esteem and prideful egotism are both most often the result of deep set, often unrecognized fears. We are afraid that if we try to become that person we aspire to be we may fail, meet with disapproval, lose friends, lose money, or perhaps we're just afraid of the unknown. Who I am now may not be great; I may not be thrilled with my life, but at least I am familiar with it. People are afraid to take a chance, make a change, even in the way they think about the universe or the way they view themselves.

Romans 12:2 instructs us: *Do not conform to the pattern of this world, but be transformed by the renewing of your mind. Then you will be able to test and approve what God's will is—his good, pleasing and perfect will.* (NIV) How many of us have truly been transformed by changing how we think about God, the universe, ourselves, and our relationship to God, others, and the world around us? How many of us can truly say that we have been transformed, changed from the inside out? I have heard of people who have experienced a "Saul on the road to Damascus" or "Ebenezer Scrooge" instance, where they were visited by a supernatural power or reached an epiphany that metamorphosed them into a new, better human being. Others have overcome addictions, or turned from a life of crime to one of service. For some the changing from selfish to altruistic happens more slowly over time, but even for those of us who have accomplished a major change in our lifestyle, have we really changed how we think, believe, and view ourselves and the world around us? The world says, "Money, fame, possessions, and power over others are the things that make you great and important; these are what you should seek." The world says, "Get back at those who have wronged you–make them pay. If you have to step on others to get to the top of the heap, that's alright, as long as you arrive on top." But the Bible teaches, *You say, 'I am rich; I have acquired wealth and do not need a thing.' But you do not realize that you are wretched, pitiful, poor, blind and naked.* (Revelation 3:17, NIV) *Jesus called them together and said, "You know that those who are regarded as rulers of the Gentiles lord it over them, and their high officials exercise authority over them. Not so with you. Instead, whoever wants to become great among you must be your servant, and whoever wants to be first must be slave of all.* (Mark 10:42-44, NIV) Do we allow ourselves to consider diverse possibilities, alternate views of reality, or the nature of the universe and our place in it? Do we view our world through the loving eyes of Abba or those of mortals? If we ever hope to achieve enlightenment, we must unlearn what we have learned from the world so that we may be filled with true wisdom from the Father.

There is a certain individual frequently in the news who has much money, influence, and holds a position of import. The world sees him as wealthy and powerful, but when I witness his detestable decrees and actions, I perceive him as wretched, pitiful, poor, blind, and naked. Most people either love him or hate him, but I pity him. When I consider the angry scowl and disgruntled frown that are etched into his visage, I doubt he has ever known true joy, peace, or love in his entire existence. We all have the same opportunities to decide which actions to take, which path to choose, and evidently he has spent his life making all the wrong choices. True, he acquired wealth and position, but at what cost? *What good is it for someone to gain the whole world, yet forfeit their soul?* (Mark 8:36, NIV) Although he lives in a gilded palace, he is a prisoner of lust, fear, and greed. A prison, no matter how ornately it is adorned, is still a prison. I do not have much money and am not in charge of any other person, yet I feel the very force of creation itself flowing through me, bolding declaring "It is well," regardless of my circumstance. I know joy, peace, love, and contentment and I am utterly free. So I neither envy nor resent this individual, nor am I compelled to bow at his throne; I comprehend that he, too, is a child of God, howbeit one who never found The Way.

"Be the change you want to see in the world," said Mahatma Gandhi. Michael Jackson echoed the same sentiment in his song, "Man in the Mirror." "Change your thoughts and you change your world," wrote Norman Vincent Peale. Comedian Carol Burnett stated, "Only I can change my life. No one can do it for me." Nineteenth-century author and philosopher Ralph Waldo Emerson wrote, "The only person you are destined to become is the person you decide to be." When confronted with fear, remember the words of Abraham Maslow: "In any given moment we have two options: to step forward into growth or step back into safety." There is also a Chinese proverb to fit this discourse: "When the winds of change blow, some people build walls and others build windmills." Are you ready to widen your horizons, to stand up to fear, and build windmills instead of walls? Are you ready to be the change you want to see in the world?

"You were born with wings, why prefer to crawl through life?" Rumi

Who are we as human beings? A whole lot more than we think we are, but not nearly as much as we are meant to be. In John 14:12 Jesus is quoted as saying, *"Very truly I tell you, whoever believes in me will do the works I have been doing, and they will do even greater things than these, because I am going to the Father."* (NIV) But Jesus walked on water, turned water into wine, healed people, calmed storms, even raised the dead–regular people can never do those things! Well, let us consider if Jesus actually said this (and it is included in the canonized Bible) then one of two things must be true: either he lied or he told the truth. This verse is a prophecy that hasn't yet completely been realized, but we are the only ones standing in the way of its fulfillment. Why he would tell us this if he didn't intend us to operate in the world the way he did? Would he make a bogus promise? And if he was wrong in this instance, what else was he wrong about?

Recorded in the book of Acts are a few miracles performed by some of his disciples, but nothing that measures up to "greater things than these." Could it be that we just didn't get it, or somewhere between then and now lost the knowledge of how it is done? What exactly is a miracle? There are those who do not believe in miracles because science cannot prove how a certain outcome was attained. They may disbelieve accounts and consider them to be hoaxes. There are others who disbelieve science because what it tells them isn't written in ancient scriptures. Both of these groups of people are out of touch with the truth. Science was put in place by the Creator, but we don't yet know everything science can teach us. I propose that miracles are indeed real (when they aren't being faked for ill-gotten gain) and that they are the result of science which we haven't discovered yet.

Many readers may have an example of a miracle you or someone you know experienced, something that others couldn't explain. I have experienced several, but one was particularly inexplicable. My husband and I were newlyweds, and he was driving our car one night on our way to a restaurant, all goo-goo eyed in love and paying no attention to the road. He was so busy looking over at me in the passenger seat that he rolled right through the stop sign into oncoming traffic on a major four-lane street. I took a deep breath and prepared for the imminent crash; instead, we drifted slowly through all the zooming cars and trucks safely to the other side, he being oblivious the entire time. Once I realized we were still in one piece, I released my breath and instructed him to keep his eyes on the road please! Here's the thing—we should have been hit a dozen times, but no one even honked their horns. It was as if we "phased" allowing the traffic to simply pass through the same space we occupied. God is the conscious force that makes up matter; therefore, He is completely capable of rearranging atoms in such a way to allow seemingly solid objects to pass through each other and I am convinced that is what happened that day. "But why were you safe and sound when others are struck and killed?" All I can answer to that is, "It wasn't our time." My husband wasn't hot-rodding; he was love-struck. He didn't take a chance on purpose, hitting the accelerator to try to beat the traffic, nor was he driving under the influence or any other irresponsible action. He wasn't daring God to protect us or any such absurdity. When the Apostle Paul was shipwrecked on an island, he went to gather wood for a fire. In the wood pile lay a poisonous snake which bit his hand. He shook it off, went on about his business, and never suffered ill effects. Paul wasn't taking an unnecessary risk handling a snake; he wasn't tempting God or testing his favor. Nor did he panic running around hollering, "I'm going to die!" He simply lived in faith.

Sometimes miracles are the result of prayer and meditation, the aligning of our hearts with God's and our steadfast belief that the prayer has been answered. Sometimes God works in the universe in ways that benefit us because it isn't our time to die and we may never know about it. But didn't Jesus say *we* would do the things he did and greater?

I believe in two crucial sciences that to date have not been completely explored or understood. First, I believe that for every action there is an equal and opposite reaction, as declared by Sir Isaac Newton. Einstein proved that matter could be transformed into energy, and we use energy derived this way from nuclear power plants all over the world today. But the inverse must also be true—there must be a way to transform energy into matter. We don't know how to do that yet, but logically it must follow that it can be done. What if it turns out that isn't something we do externally, but internally? What if it is with our minds and hearts that we can use energy in and from our own bodies to create matter such as a protective shield or a healthy organ? I'm not a doctor or a scientist, but the logic is sound; if matter can be transformed into energy (and it can), then it must follow that energy can be transformed into matter.

Second is the potential lying within the science of compassion. *Jesus went through all the towns and villages, teaching in their synagogues, proclaiming the good news of the kingdom and healing every disease and sickness. When he saw the crowds, he had compassion on them, because they were harassed and helpless, like sheep without a shepherd.* (Matthew 9:35-36, NIV) *When Jesus landed and saw a large crowd, he had compassion on them and healed their sick.* (Matthew 14:14, NIV) *Jesus called his disciples to him and said, "I have compassion for these people; they have already been with me three days and have nothing to eat"* (Matthew 15:32, NIV) and he went on to divide the five loaves and two fish to feed the crowd of over 15,000. *Jesus had compassion on them and touched their eyes. Immediately they received their sight and followed him.* (Matthew 20:34, NIV)

I'm sure you noticed the common thread; Jesus had compassion on the people, then he performed a miracle. There is phenomenal power in compassion, a power that few humans have ever fully tapped. Could it be that it was this great compassion that gave Jesus the ability to heal and feed people? Was it his compassion that allowed him to perform an indefinable miracle through his death and resurrection? Do we have the capacity to operate in that same measure of compassion? If you believe the words of Jesus to be true, then you must also believe that we have the potential to do things beyond science's current ability to explain, and I think compassion is one of the keys.

Therefore, as God's chosen people, holy and dearly loved, clothe yourselves with compassion, kindness, humility, gentleness and patience. (Colossians 3:12, NIV) *Be kind and compassionate to one another, forgiving each other, just as in Christ God forgave you.* (Ephesians 4:32, NIV) "Compassion and tolerance are not a sign of weakness, but a sign of strength." (Dalai Lama) "If you want to be happy, practice compassion. If you want to be happy, practice compassion." (Dalai Lama) "Compassion is the basis of morality." (Arthur Schopenhauer) "Converting your energy to compassion and understanding, once you accept this reality, helps our own healing; that type of energy is more positive and calming." (Lisa Kardos) "Research shows that the more compassionate we are toward ourselves, the happier we are and the more resilient we become when faced with difficult events in our lives." (Paul Gilbert, PhD) "Cultivating compassion for ourselves and others can bring balance and harmony to our lives in a way we never dreamed of." (Thubten Chodron) *Finally, all of you, be like-minded, be sympathetic, love one another, be compassionate and humble.* (1 Peter 3:8, NIV) "Compassion is at the heart of every little thing we do. It is the dearest quality we possess. Yet all too often it can be cast aside with consequences too tragic to speak of. To lose our compassion, we lose what it is to be human." Anonymous

Greed, prejudice, hatred, and fear are all things that we learn, not that we are born with. There is a theory of humanity which states we are all born in sin and have to work our way out of it or be saved from it before we can enter the kingdom of Heaven; the opposing theory postulates that new souls born into infant bodies have come straight from God's presence in the Heavenly realm, therefore they are born pure and innocent. Statements made by Jesus support the latter theory as does modern research. *And he said: "Truly I tell you, unless you change and become like little children, you will never enter the kingdom of heaven."* (Matthew 18:3, NIV) *But Jesus called the children to him and said, "Let the little children come to me, and do not hinder them, for the kingdom of God belongs to such as these. Truly I tell you, anyone who will not receive the kingdom of God like a little child will never enter it."* (Luke 18:16-17, NIV) *21 At that time Jesus, full of joy through the Holy Spirit, said, "I praise you, Father, Lord of heaven and earth, because you have hidden these things from the wise and learned, and revealed them to little children. Yes, Father, for this is what you were pleased to do.* (Luke 10:21, NIV) *"Do you hear what these children are saying?" they asked him. "Yes," replied Jesus, "have you never read, "'From the lips of children and infants you, Lord, have called forth your praise'?"* (Matthew 21:16, NIV) In the Old Testament David bears witness to this idea. *Through the praise of children and infants you have established a stronghold against your enemies, to silence the foe and the avenger.* (Psalms 8:2, NIV) And Paul wrote in 1 Corinthians 14:20: *Brothers and sisters, stop thinking like children. In regard to evil be infants, but in your thinking be adults.* (NIV)

These verses support the belief that children are not born sinful, but rather learn to think, feel, and do evil. Recent studies on empathy in small children show that even babies understand compassion. In one of these, a researcher would be in a room with a toddler as young as eighteen months who was happily playing with toys or in a ball pit when the researcher would drop something and say aloud, "Uh-oh!" At that universal clue, the toddlers would look to see what was wrong. The researcher would then stretch a hand unsuccessfully toward the object that was just out of reach. Almost every toddler without hesitation and without being asked, left the toys, came over with a big smile, picked up the dropped item, and handed it to the researcher. The desire to help someone else is an inborn trait that must be squelched before that tender heart hardens. Another experiment which included even younger babies involved two hand-puppets operated by the researcher. He or she would act out a short puppet show for the child in which one puppet was kind, and the other was mean. After the skit, the researcher would hold out both puppets to the baby. Regardless of which puppet played which role or their physical colors and characteristics, the vast majority of subjects picked the kind puppet instead of the mean one. They documented that four out of five three-month-olds chose the nice puppet. Even a three-month-old can identify the difference between kindness and malice and choose kindness! At what point along the way does this compassion that God placed in our hearts at birth get lost? This is why Jesus directed us to become like little children; we have to unlearn all the wrong thoughts, feelings, and actions we picked up along the way. We must rediscover the essence of who we were created to be.

It is commonly stated that humans only use about ten percent of their brains; technically that is not true. Much of the brain's function is automatic and occurring all the time, whether we are awake or asleep. What is true, however, is that much of our thought and imaginative potential goes untapped. But what about the potential power of our hearts? What portion of our heart energy is left unexplored and unused? We are just beginning to understand the dynamic influence our hearts have on our bodies and the surrounding universe. With feelings created in the heart we commune with Adonia, send healing agents flowing through our bodies, convey signals to plants, animals, and other people, affect the weather, perceive our own realities, and perhaps release a compassion so vibrant as to perform the miraculous. It is in the feeling and acts of compassion that we as human beings reach our highest potential; it is in expressions of compassion that the One who is Alpha and Omega truly lives through us and we in Him.

CONCLUSION

These are the things I think about all day long. Much of these concepts and ideas came to me in a short period of time and I struggled to organize them properly for sharing. There's more, but this is enough to start with. By practicing principles found in this text, my health has improved and peace and joy fill my days. There are times, I must admit, when traffic frustrates me. Some driver pulls in front of me and slows down, a car on the off ramp can't decide whether to speed up and pull in front of me, slow down to get behind, or just drive alongside until he runs out of the ramp, or other drivers won't let me change lanes when I need to (don't want a truck in front of me!) I can get a little agitated but then I think, "Is that worth losing my peace over? Is traffic worth giving away my joy?" and my feelings settle back down into their normal rhythm of contented gratitude. I listen to my music and view the scenery with appreciation flowing from me to the Universal Spirit, but sometimes I want to know what's going on in the world. I turn on the news to hear of a new disaster or tragedy and my heart goes out to the victims in compassion. But I must confess that righteous anger rises up in me when I hear of the inhumane, cruel, and detestable acts some people perpetrate upon others. I am enraged by injustices that those in power commit, allow or encourage, and sometimes my soul grieves exceedingly because of the hatred and violence that permeates our species. I think, "God had every reason to allow the flood to destroy what he made and I'm totally surprised that He hasn't brought another punishment down on us." Then I remember that God is love; He is compassion. He sees the offender as a beloved child who has lost her way, or maybe never really found it. I am reminded that I am to love the unlovable, even the mean-spirited and the oppressor. I allow myself to feel anger at the offense, but I understand that me being mad about something doesn't solve anything; it only coils my DNA up in tight, little knots doing harm to my own body and soul. So I have to release the anger and instead take action. That action may be to write or call my representatives in government, donate time or money to a worthy cause, write an encouraging letter to someone affected, compose a song or poem, pray, meditate, and create a little more peace in my corner of the world. By performing random acts of kindness, we can impact our world, pushing back the darkness by shining the light of love.

When I was growing up my mother constantly reminded me of Jesus' words in Luke 12:48, *"To whom much is given, much is required."* That ingrained teaching compels me to write the words in this text and to share what has been shared with me. I am still learning, still taking steps toward that next level of glory, eagerly anticipating the ensuing revelation. I may not have gotten everything I wrote here exactly right, and it could be that in the coming months and years as we collectively learn more from science, nature, and Abba Himself that some of what I have penned will become obsolete. Until that time I will continue to seek my God, to know and love Him more, to explore the possibilities He has laid before me, to expand the potential of my heart, and to embody compassion to the best of my ability. All glory, honor, and praise be to our Creator and Lord, He who is Love eternal, who inhabits all, connects all, and contains all of the all, forever and ever, Amen!

Printed in the United States
By Bookmasters